BASES LOADED

ADVANCE PRAISE FOR *BASES LOADED*

"Trump focused his campaign—and his presidency—on appealing to his political base. Instead of winning new converts, he focuses on maintaining enthusiasm in his base. Panagopoulos shows us that Trump's actions are not unique but are the product of the nature of campaigns in the twenty-first century. To do so, Panagopoulos deftly integrates voter opinion and behavior, campaign strategy, and the nature of new media in the age of Big Data."

—**JOHN ALDRICH**, *Pfizer, Inc./Edmund T. Pratt, Jr. University Distinguished Professor of Political Science, Duke University*

"Panagopoulos has produced a clear, comprehensive, and detailed overview of the dramatic changes in the ways presidential campaigns are conducted in today's era of deep partisan polarization. He explains why modern presidential campaigns focus primarily on identifying and turning out partisans rather than persuading swing voters. This book will be a valuable resource for scholars, students, and practitioners of American elections and voting behavior."

—**ALAN ABRAMOWITZ**, *Alben W. Barkley Professor of Political Science, Emory University*

BASES LOADED

How U.S. Presidential Campaigns Are Changing and Why It Matters

COSTAS PANAGOPOULOS

OXFORD
UNIVERSITY PRESS

OXFORD
UNIVERSITY PRESS

Oxford University Press is a department of the University of Oxford. It furthers
the University's objective of excellence in research, scholarship, and education
by publishing worldwide. Oxford is a registered trade mark of Oxford University
Press in the UK and certain other countries.

Published in the United States of America by Oxford University Press
198 Madison Avenue, New York, NY 10016, United States of America.

Library of Congress Cataloging-in-Publication Data
Names: Panagopoulos, Costas, author.
Title: Bases loaded : how U.S. presidential campaigns are changing and
why it matters / Costas Panagopoulos.
Description: New York, NY : Oxford University Press, [2021] |
Includes bibliographical references and index.
Identifiers: LCCN 2020022034 (print) | LCCN 2020022035 (ebook) |
ISBN 9780197533062 (hardback) | ISBN 9780197533079 (paperback) |
ISBN 9780197533093 (epub)
Subjects: LCSH: Presidents—United States—Election. | United States—Politics and
government—21st century. | Partisanship—Political aspects—United States.
Classification: LCC JK528 .P36 2021 (print) | LCC JK528 (ebook) |
DDC 324.70973—dc23
LC record available at https://lccn.loc.gov/2020022034
LC ebook record available at https://lccn.loc.gov/2020022035

9 8 7 6 5 4 3 2 1

Paperback printed by Sheridan Books, Inc., United States of America
Hardback printed by Bridgeport National Bindery, Inc., United States of America

—With limitless love, for my son—
George Ruggiero Panagopoulos

CONTENTS

FIGURES

ACKNOWLEDGMENTS

This book has been in development for many years. As fate would have it, it was completed thanks in large part to the support provided by my family just as the COVID-19 health crisis was erupting in the United States. To my husband, Mark Ruggiero, and to my mother, Vasiliki Panagopoulos, who generously helped care for our one-year-old son, George, while I finalized the project, I am eternally indebted.

The book was initially inspired by a paper I presented at a workshop on "Voter Mobilization in Context" organized by Professors John Aldrich (Duke University) and Rachel Gibson (University of Manchester) held at the University of Manchester (UK) on November 8, 2013. I was honored to be invited by John and Rachel to present this work at the gathering, and the project benefited from invaluable input from workshop participants. An updated version of the initial paper was published in a themed special issue of *Party Politics* guest edited by Aldrich and Gibson. I am grateful for thoughtful and constructive feedback provided by the editors and anonymous reviewers during the peer review process for this article. Some of the ideas and material reflected in this book originated in the article titled, "All About

That Base: Changing Campaign Strategies in U.S. Presidential Elections," published in *Party Politics* in September 2015.

In the years since, I have been fortunate to work with several talented, skilled, and dedicated research assistants to develop the exposition and analyses that comprise the current volume. These have included two exceptional postdoctoral research assistants, Benjamin Farrer and Kyle Endres, who provided assistance while I was on the faculty at Fordham University. At Northeastern University, I benefited from the generosity and technical expertise of Tim Fraser, a doctoral student in the Department of Political Science, who provided exemplary assistance. All three of these individuals worked tirelessly to help shape the analyses included in the book, and I am indebted to them all for their patience, contributions, and professionalism. I also thank Sasha Volodarsky and Austin Barraza for their assistance.

I also benefited from suggestions provided by David McBride, editor-in-chief (social science), and the two anonymous referees who reviewed the manuscript for Oxford University Press. I appreciate their input and support.

I am indebted to several colleagues for providing helpful insights or data at various stages of this project. These include, first and foremost, my longtime collaborator and dear friend Donald Green (Columbia University) who was also a participant at the original workshop in Manchester. The project also benefited from research I conducted while I was visiting professor of Political Science and a fellow at the Center for the Study of American Politics at Yale University (2015–2016), and I thank Alan Gerber for his generosity, hospitality, and support. I also thank John Aldrich, Rachel Gibson, Ed Fieldhouse, David Mayhew, Alan Abramowitz, Whit Ayres, Karl Rove, and Robby Mook for their support, feedback, and encouragement. Multiple conversations about the project with my former Fordham University colleagues Jeffrey Cohen and Richard Fleisher, as well as with Robert Erikson, Aaron Weinschenk, David

Nickerson, William Mayer, David Rochefort, Nick Beauchamp, Woody Kay, and several other colleagues at Northeastern University (where I presented an abridged version of this book at the "President's Day" lecture in February 2020), also helped shape my thinking about the project. In addition, the analyses in Chapter 6 would not have been possible without the generosity and support of Travis Ridout and Darrell West who shared their data with me and kindly endured endless questions and special requests. Their patience, generosity, and willingness to be helpful have been inspiring, and this project is stronger because of their help.

Finally, I thank Holly Mitchell and Preetham Raj and the rest of the production team at Oxford University Press for their timeliness, diligence, and professionalism.

Any errors of omission or commission, however, are purely my own.

Costas Panagopoulos
Boston, MA

INTRODUCTION

If all goes according to plan, Trump could lose the whole swing vote and still win the election.

— BRIAN WALSH, *Trump SuperPAC America First Action*
(quoted in Miller et al. 2019)

People trying to persuade swing voters are probably wasting their time because nearly all voters have already put their jersey on.

— CHRIS WILSON, *GOP Strategist (quoted in Miller et al. 2019)*

THESE STATEMENTS BY STRATEGISTS WORKING to re-elect President Donald J. Trump in 2020 represent a sea change in political campaign strategy that is hard to overstate. Even as recently as the 1980s or 1990s, the notion that swing or persuadable voters could be viewed as inconsequential or dispensable in election outcomes would have been inconceivable. Famed George W. Bush strategist Karl Rove remarked, "[t]he strategy was never one of simply looking at identifying red Republicans and getting them out to vote; it was also a campaign of addition and persuasion" (Miller, Burnett, and Fram 2019). But things have changed in recent years, and swing voters are increasingly taking a back seat to partisans in political campaigns, including presidential campaigns, whose calculations suggest focusing on these voters may suffice to secure victory. The 2000 election was a watershed year in this transition. In that cycle, Matthew Dowd, campaign strategist for the Bush campaign in 2000, observed that "the fraction of the electorate genuinely

Bases Loaded. Costas Panagopoulos, Oxford University Press (2021). © Oxford University Press.
DOI: 10.1093/oso/9780197533062.001.0001.

open to persuasion had shrunk since 1980 from 22 percent to 7 percent" (Baker 2014: 89). These figures suggested to Dowd that persuadable voters were not necessarily a decisive bloc. He later recalled realizing the campaign, "could lose the 6 or 7 percent and win the election, which was fairly revolutionary, because everybody up until that time had said, 'Swing voters, swing voters, swing voters, swing voters, swing voters'" (Baker 2014: 89). Ultimately, Dowd concluded, "the long-sought-after 'swing voters' were a vanishing breed in American politics," and the campaign made a strategic decision not to move to the center but to court the Republican base more aggressively instead (Baker 2014: 88).

Despite oft-heard public outcries about access to lavish, seemingly limitless funds, political campaigns generally operate with finite resources, and they have incentives to be strategic in how to allocate those resources to maximize impact (Panagopoulos 2017; Panagopoulos 2015). One of the most important decisions campaigns must make is to determine which voters to target with their efforts. In doing so, strategists must grapple with decades worth of research that suggests campaigns have only limited capacity to influence voters, especially in terms of shaping their preferences (Lazarsfeld, Berelson, and Gaudet 1944). Preferences can, and often do, change over the course of a campaign, but typically slowly and not by very much (Erikson and Wlezien 2012). While swing voters require both persuasion and then mobilization, sympathetic partisans typically only need to be coaxed into voting on Election Day. Over the past few decades, and especially since the 2000 election cycle, presidential campaigns have increasingly turned their attention away from swing voters, opting instead to concentrate their efforts on partisans predisposed to supporting their parties or candidates in the first place. I view the focus on mobilizing committed partisans primarily as a *base maximization* strategy, while efforts to recruit additional support via conversion or persuasion from voters without partisan affinities can be considered a *base expansion* approach. The evidence presented in this book documents the shift in the strategic focus of presidential campaigns from base expansion to base maximization and links these developments to technological and other changes that have transformed how political campaigns operate. This strategic recalibration has had important implications for democracy in America. The consequences have been striking, affecting both the composition of the electorate and the levels of partisan polarization in the United States.

The basic argument advanced throughout can be summarized as follows: Motivated to allocate resources with efficacy and efficiency in pursuit of victory, campaigns in recent cycles have harnessed refinements in targeting capabilities to increasingly direct their attention to base partisans, relative to swing, persuadable, or independent voters. In other words, campaigns have increasingly prioritized base maximization over base expansion strategies in their efforts over the past few decades. The greater emphasis on base partisans has boosted their participation in recent elections, widening the disparities in participation rates between committed partisans and voters with weaker partisan attachments. These growing disparities have likely strengthened partisan polarization in the United States.

A big part of this story has to do with developments in campaign technology, most notably the development of microtargeting, big data, and predictive analytics, over the past few decades. Microtargeting has revolutionized how campaigns identify, target, and communicate with voters (Panagopoulos 2017; Panagopoulos 2015). Hillygus and Shields (2008) have convincingly shown how microtargeting can be used to pursue persuadable voters in campaigns, but microtargeting tactics can be deployed just as easily to home in on partisans or other voter types with comparable precision. Such fundamental changes in the machinery of political campaigns do not come along often, but they can have important consequences. These capabilities become all the more important for political campaigns as elections become more competitive. In recent years, presidential general elections have been decided by ever-shrinking margins. This trend is illustrated in Figure 1.1, which plots the major-party popular vote margin in presidential elections between 1956 and 2016. The overall pattern is clear: The popular vote spread has dwindled over time, with the most recent cycles routinely decided by margins below 5 percentage points.

When elections are this close, campaigns may reason they can succeed by focusing almost exclusively on mobilizing committed partisans. Asked in an interview in 2004 whether it was mathematically possible to win a presidential race without any swing voters, GOP strategist Karl Rove, whose nicknames

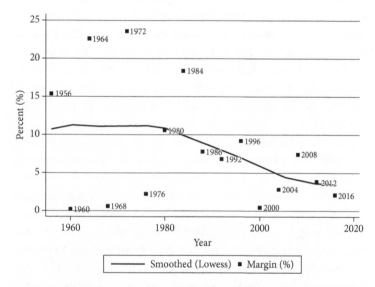

FIGURE 1.1 Major-Party Vote Margin, Presidential Elections (1956–2016)
Source: Compiled by author.

included "Bush's brain," did not skip a beat: "Yes," he replied, quickly adding, "[b]ut I think that's a very risky strategy" (Kornblut 2004). Political scientist Alan Abramowitz (2015) has observed that the two major-party bases are roughly equal in size and loyalty, which tends to make elections highly competitive at the national level and fuels the intensity of partisan conflict. This reasoning is justified given the burgeoning number of studies that show the swing voter population has declined in recent elections (Jones 2008; Dimock, Clark, and Horowitz 2008; Abramowitz 2011; Campbell 2016), so the pool of voters available for persuasion is shrinking. At the same time, the parties' respective partisan bases appear to be growing. As I show in Chapter 3, the number of Americans who identify as strong partisans has grown steadily since 1956, mainly due to intensifying attachments to the Republican Party, while the number of pure independents—the most persuadable voters— has been on the decline.

Persuasion is also unreliable (Zaller 1992; Kalla and Broockman 2018), costly (Green and Gerber 2012), and difficult to achieve (Kalla and Broockman 2018; Nickerson 2005; Bailey, Hopkins, and Rogers 2016). Even when campaigns manage to jolt voter preferences successfully, the effects generally last no longer than a few days, at best, before vote intentions return to equilibrium levels (Gerber et al. 2011). By contrast, as I discuss in Chapter 3, partisans are more reliable, increasingly reluctant to cross party lines to vote for the opposition (Hetherington 2001; Miller 1991). Additionally, a flurry of research in recent years provides an abundance of insights about how voters can be mobilized effectively (Green and Gerber 2012), especially if it is not first necessary to persuade them which candidate to support.

In the chapters that follow, I explore these trends more thoroughly and rigorously and consider their social and political implications more fully. The focus is decidedly on presidential elections, in part because, as high-salience, well-funded, and relatively centralized national affairs, the changes I describe are likely to manifest most clearly, but similar paradigm shifts have likely materialized in other types of campaigns, including congressional midterms and even state or local races.

In large part, the empirical analyses rely on data obtained from the American National Election Studies (ANES) conducted in presidential years between 1956 and 2016.[1] These data are admittedly imperfect; for example, the questions may not be as detailed or as precise as one might like for certain variables, modes of data collection have changed over the years, and the sample sizes are not always abundant. The analyses are also almost entirely observational, so causal interpretations are unwise. But the ANES data do offer some advantages in terms of continuity and enable explorations over time that serve the central purposes of this study. These data are supplemented with additional sources as available throughout in order to extend the analyses beyond the scope of the ANES.

The remainder of the book is organized as follows. Chapter 2 describes developments in campaign technology, focusing on advances in microtargeting capabilities and explaining why the presidential election in 2000 represents a watershed moment in this process.

Chapter 3 investigates both the timing of presidential vote choice and the rates of party support and party defection in recent presidential elections. The percentage of voters who are making their decision to support one presidential candidate instead of the other after the general election campaign is shrinking. Campaigns struggle to persuade voters once they've reached a decision to vote for a particular candidate. This is an added motivation for campaigns to focus on mobilization instead of persuasion. Voters are not only making up their minds earlier than ever, but they are also more loyal than ever. Partisans, particularly strong partisans, rarely defect from supporting their party's nominee, which was not the case in presidential elections just a few decades ago.

Chapter 4 demonstrates the change in campaign-targeting strategies both over time and following the adoption of microtargeting techniques by political operatives leading up to and following the 2000 election. The analyses show that strong partisans and committed ideologues have been targeted by campaigns at higher rates, while independents have received less and less attention from campaigns in recent cycles. I concede these analyses represent only an indirect attempt to observe shifts in presidential campaign strategy, but consistent, direct, and reliable measures of campaign targeting over time are unavailable. Nevertheless, inferences about campaign behavior and strategic decision-making can be gleaned from Americans' reports of campaign activity.

Chapter 5 advances a direct examination of presidential campaign strategies by analyzing the contents of presidential advertisements broadcasted on television in recent cycles. The analyses are suggestive and largely explorative, but they suggest overall that presidential campaigns have increasingly featured partisan cues in their appeals on television, presumably to activate latent predispositions among partisans in their camps and to trigger the salience of social identity processes rooted in partisan identification. I interpret this evidence to support the notion of a base maximizing strategy as opposed to base expansion efforts.

Chapter 6 begins to consider the implications of the shift toward base maximization in recent presidential campaign cycles by examining patterns in voter turnout among partisan subgroups in the electorate. The analyses show that persuadable voters are voting at lower rates while strong partisans are voting at higher rates in recent presidential elections. These patterns have fundamentally changed the nature of the electorate, which has been comprised increasingly of strong partisans in recent years, relative to independent, swing, or persuadable voters.

Chapter 7 examines one of the potential implications of this shift in targeting strategies: its effects on partisan polarization. Over the last few decades, elected officials have grown further apart based on the voting records of members of Congress. On some measures, the mass public has also grown further apart. Each party's shift toward disproportionately communicating with their base has likely exacerbated and accelerated both mass and elite polarization. Using a common measure of elite polarization, the analyses reveal a marked shift following the 2000 election that, at a minimum, coincides with the changes in overall campaign strategies documented in the book.

The concluding chapter summarizes the key findings reported in the book and provides some additional reflections on the implications for politics and democracy in America.

BIG DATA AND OTHER

BIG CHANGES

Big Data revolutionized the way American politicians win elections.

In the process, it broke American politics.

—TODD AND DANN (2017)

"The art of politics is moving closer to a science. Whichever party has the best Big Data is likely to have the most Big Wins."

—KARL ROVE (2019)

IF YOU ARE CURRENTLY ONE of the 240 million voting-age Americans, you can likely find yourself listed in the national database maintained by the progressive campaign data behemoth Catalist, alongside detailed information including your address, date of birth, gender, ethnicity, phone number, party registration status, your history of voting in election cycles dating back for decades—and up to 700 other pieces of information, like whether you own a boat, a cat, or a dog; are an automotive enthusiast; whether you are interested in crafts or photography or gardening; even whether your home has air conditioning or a pool (Hersh 2015). Some of this information is compiled by elections officials in local jurisdictions, who, since passage of the 2002 Help America Vote Act, have been required to maintain electronic databases of registered voters in all states except

Bases Loaded. Costas Panagopoulos, Oxford University Press (2021). © Oxford University Press.
DOI: 10.1093/oso/9780197533062.001.0001.

North Dakota (which does not require registration). Other details are collected by commercial vendors who track this information for nonpolitical purposes but make it available to political parties and campaigns for purchase to augment their databases and to create more refined voter profiles. Political parties and campaigns then mine and exploit this information using sophisticated statistical techniques to estimate how likely any individual voter is to vote, support or oppose a specific policy position, be responsive to a direct-mail solicitation by a presidential candidate, volunteer to knock on doors, convince their coworkers or spouses to support a candidate, post a message supporting a candidate on Facebook, or even change their mind to support a different candidate in the election. These propensity scores are then used by campaigns to figure out which voters should be targeted and how—and even which could be overlooked entirely when resources are scarce and must be allocated strategically to maximize impact.

In a nutshell, this is microtargeting. The technique is fueled by the availability of big data and leverages predictive analytics and other statistical modeling techniques to make data-driven decisions about campaign strategy and tactics. Recently, campaign data analysts have turned increasingly to more sophisticated modeling approaches that rely on data mining and supervised and unsupervised machine learning algorithms, like decision trees, to classify and target voters (Nickerson and Rogers 2014). Microtargeting, big data, and predictive analytics have transformed political campaigns over the past two decades, not because these techniques caused campaigns to target their efforts—political campaigns had traditionally targeted voters and allocated resources strategically (Shaw 2006; Panagopoulos 2017; Panagopoulos and Weinschenk 2015)—but because these new technologies enabled campaigns to target voters with greater accuracy and precision than ever before—and at the individual level. Prior to the advent of precision targeting, political campaigns had to rely on more aggregated, macro-level approaches, like geographic, precinct- or group-based targeting (Burton, Miller, and Shea 2015), that were more crude, less reliable, and potentially wasteful and counterproductive.

Microtargeting is essentially a marketing and advertising technique that originated in the commercial sphere (Ridout 2009). Even today, most of its practitioners are businesses and corporations seeking more efficient ways to promote their products and services to their clientele. Targeted advertising and marketing in the private sector was an extension of the customer-relationship management model adopted in the late 1970s by corporations like Nordstrom. Predictive modeling had been used to create credit scores since the 1970s and had been adopted for direct marketing purposes since the 1980s thanks in large part to sizable amounts of consumer data collected by companies like Acxiom, Epsilon, and InfoUSA (Nielsen 2012: 140). It was a fully-fledged paradigm by the 1990s (Kasanoff, Rogers, and Peppers 2001). Firms were determined to make the most of the dictum that 80 percent of profits come from 20 percent of customers, and customer-relationship management allowed companies to do this partly by recording and tracking consumer purchases. The most common commercial use of this information was to segment the entire list of customers by the frequency, regularity, and monetary value of their purchases. By identifying customers who made the most frequent purchases, were in the store most regularly, and spent the most money, businesses could identify their best customers. A central goal, from that point on, was to provide special treatment to those consumers.

Another important use of this information was to make projections about future consumption behavior. Previously, these predictions were made at aggregated or group levels— a product might sell well among men, for example, and so it would be marketed more intensively toward these consumers.

But with the ability to track every customer individually, companies no longer had to rely on such highly aggregated guessing. Consumers' actual, individual histories of consumer behavior could be used to tailor commercial appeals, so not all individuals from the same demographic group had to be marketed to in the same way. This represented a sea change that, when applied to political campaigns, became known as microtargeting.

The process of microtargeting in politics and business is similar and shares many goals, but the starting point is different. Businesses build their own databases of customers and must track purchases and other attributes and behavior. In some ways, political campaigns begin with a head start because comprehensive lists of registered voters are compiled by elections officials and they contain many (even most) of the critical variables campaigns need to predict political attitudes and behavior. For example, eight states record voters' race; thirty states allow voters to officially register with a political party and include this information in their files; twenty-eight states, including seventeen of the thirty states that have party registration, keep records of the party primaries in which individuals previously cast ballots. Voter files also include voters' turnout histories. The information available in publicly maintained voter files can also be supplemented with information obtained from other sources, including commercial vendors, government agencies (like the Federal Elections Commission, which tracks individual contributions above $200 to federal candidates), and political campaigns or parties themselves. Microtargeting also allows campaigns to collect information from small universes of voters—such as polls or surveys of limited samples of voters that probe respondents about issue priorities and preferences or experimental tests designed to compare the effectiveness of one message versus another—and to use statistical techniques to extrapolate the results to individual voters in much broader electorates (Hersh 2015; Nickerson and Rogers 2014; Panagopoulos 2017). In the end, much of the psychographic information about lifestyle choices, interests, or apolitical activities, while interesting, rarely improves the predictive accuracy of statistical models estimated to make predictions about political attitudes and behaviors, but two variables generally available from voter files—party affiliation and turnout history—prove to be very useful to campaigns (Hersh 2015). Past turnout is highly predictive of future turnout (Plutzer 2002; Nickerson and Rogers 2014), and party affiliation is highly predictive of vote choice (see Chapter 1; Smidt 2017; Miller 1991). These two pieces of information alone can help campaigns go a long way in deciphering which voters are ripe for mobilization or persuasion, which will likely vote for them without any prodding, and which voters to completely avoid.

Some of the information described earlier, along with detailed Census information, had been collected and available to campaigns for decades before the microtargeting revolution, but campaigns rarely fully exploited it. Democrats began to systematically encourage state parties to build large-scale databases of voters in the late 1980s, but only thirty states had centralized, digital lists available by 2002 (Nielsen 2012). For years, mail vendors were at the cutting edge of using consumer data for modeling purposes and at least a decade ahead of the political campaign learning curve (Malchow 2003). Part of the reason is technology. As Nickerson and Rogers (2014: 52) explain, "adequate storage and computing power required large investments that were beyond the infrastructure of nearly all campaigns and state parties." But "perhaps the biggest impediment to wider adoption of data-driven campaigning," note the authors, "was simply that statistical thinking—and the human capital that produces it—had not yet taken root in the world of political consulting" (Nickerson and Rogers 2014: 52).

THE 2000 ELECTION: A TURNING POINT

By the turn of the millennium, things had started to change. Microtargeting techniques had gradually expanded in the political sphere throughout the 1980s and 1990s (Howard 2006), when it was used initially for fundraising purposes but eventually also for voter contact through direct-mail programs (Nielsen 2012). In 1996, President Clinton's re-election campaign used customer-relationship-management techniques, in minor but important ways, to win back the moderate voters who had deserted the Democratic Party in the 1994 midterm elections.

The strategic context facing Republicans in 2000, and the need to mobilize base supporters in particular, led the party to deploy sophisticated microtargeting tactics. Rudimentary persuasion microtargeting strategies had been used effectively by the Clinton campaigns in the 1990s (Hillygus and Shields 2008), and Republicans, defeated in the 1996 election, were eager to leverage new and emerging technologies for electoral gain. In 1996, Bob Dole, the Republican nominee, had been criticized as an old-fashioned candidate who was reluctant to match Clinton's use of technology and unwilling to abandon the traditional persuasion template. After his defeat in 1996, the national party elite became more conservative (McCarty et al. 2006) just as the voters were becoming more evangelical (Pierson and Skocpol 2007). Throughout the 1990s, every incoming cohort of the U.S. House of Representatives had been more conservative than the last (Pierson et al. 2007). Similarly, by 2000, most citizen activists in the Republican Party were more conservative than they had been in previous elections, and this trend, combined with the trend toward elite polarization (McCarty et al. 2008), constituted a powerful set of incentives for a base mobilization campaign. Hillygus and Shields (2008: 149) acknowledge this in quoting Jacob Hacker and Paul Pierson:

> What is the great force that pulls Republican politicians to the right? In a word, the "base.". . . The base has always had power, but never the kind of power it has today. With money more important in elections than ever, the base has money. With the political and organizational resources of ordinary voters in decline, the base is mobilized and well-organized.

A confluence of factors, however, made the 2000 election cycle a major turning point (Pierson and Skocpol 2007). Developments in marketing, strategic considerations facing Republicans, and institutional changes in the regulatory environments surrounding both data management and campaign finance all played a role. But it was pioneers like Alexander Gage, who coined the term "microtargeting" in 2002, that inspired a tectonic shift in the adoption of the techniques for politics. In the 2000 cycle, Gage convinced Karl Rove, the chief strategist for the George W. Bush campaign (latter dubbed by Bush as "the architect" of his victory), that microtargeting could be applied to politics and would lead to a Bush victory (Wayne 2008). Rove concurred, and microtargeting tactics featured prominently in the campaign, ultimately helping lead George W. Bush to victory, largely by identifying and targeting likely supporters. At the time, focusing so heavily on the base represented a break from conventional wisdom and was, by all accounts, a gamble (Kornblut 2004). Howard (2006) makes the case that the 2000 election marked the first occasion when new technologies were not just complementing old methods, or subtly changing these old methods via integration, but instead were the centerpiece of a campaign strategy aimed at mobilizing existing partisans. Abramson, Aldrich, and Rohde (2002) come to a similar conclusion, showing that the Bush campaign also drove turnout up among the demographic groups traditionally thought of as representing the Republican base. Ridout, Goldstein, and Feltus (2012) echo this view and find empirical support for this interpretation when evaluating the television advertising strategies of the campaigns. The Republicans focused their television ads on the base. The authors observe, "[a]ll told, the results suggest that one particular feature of the 2000 air war was a more focused appeal to Republican viewers on the part of Bush, with Gore doing less to target particular partisans" (Ridout et al. 2012: 17).

Other developments contributed to creating a turning point in 2000. Changes in the regulatory environment helped make microtargeting more feasible. Kizza (2013) describes important institutional changes that fed into the confluence of circumstances producing the base-mobilization-campaign template. He argues that an attempt to prevent financial institutions from sharing personal information with third parties, the Gramm–Leach–Bliley Financial Services Modernization Act, passed on November 12, 1999, actually had the opposite effect. "This one Act has opened a door for these companies to merge and consolidate customer data from several sources," Kizza explained (2013: 89). Although the Choicepoint scandal in 2000 led to increased calls for tighter regulation of consumer data, this gap in the regulatory framework allowed consultants to get particularly creative in 2000. As Schier (2000: 96) noted, "[f]ew Americans [had] heard of database management firms, and little [did] unsuspecting citizens realize how much information about them these companies collect[ed] for campaign use."

Major transformations in the media and communications landscape were underway at roughly the same period and had profound implications for how political campaigns could reach out to specific voters in targeted ways (Panagopoulos 2009b). While the first email was sent by developers at MIT in 1965, it was not until the late 1990s that email became commonly used (Gibbs 2016). Outlook and AOL launched in 1993, Hotmail in 1996, and Yahoo! in 1997, but it was not until 1998 that "email was cemented in the public consciousness" (Gibbs 2016). In politics, Jesse Ventura's independent campaign for governor in Minnesota pioneered the use of email in 1998 (Panagopoulos 2009b), but email was still in its nascent political phase at the time. By the 2000 election, email enjoyed widespread use for the first time during a presidential campaign. In the GOP presidential primary in 2000, candidate John McCain had considerable success with fundraising online (Panagopoulos 2009b). Blogs and net-organized events (MeetUp.com) came onto the political scene in 2003 and 2004 (and were used heavily by Howard Dean's Democratic campaign for president in that cycle), and social networking sites like MySpace and YouTube emerged in 2006 (Panagopoulos 2009b). While Facebook launched in 2004, it was not until Barack Obama's 2008 White House quest that it was deployed in full force in a presidential campaign (Panagopoulos 2009b). Targetable media options continued to expand over the next two decades. Advances providing details about listening and viewing habits on radio, cable, and network television, as well as audience demographics and other characteristics, matured, affording enhanced precision in targeting specific listeners or viewers even using broadcast media options. Campaigns aiming to reach audiences that skewed Democratic in 2014, for example, might have targeted snarky comedies like NBC's *Community, Saturday Night Live*, and IFC's *Portlandia*; liberal shows like Comedy Central's *The Daily Show with Jon Stewart*; HBO's *Real Time with Bill Maher* or Aaron Sorkin's *The Newsroom*; or ABC's *Scandal* or *Modern Family*. Republican viewers favored business-minded real estate shows, including HGTV's *Rent or Buy, Buying and Selling*, or *Love it or List It*; A&E's *Duck Dynasty*; and crime shows like CBS's *NCIS* and *Blue Bloods* (Hibberd 2014). In 2013, top shows among women aged 18–49 on basic cable included FX's *American Horror Story* and *Sons of Anarchy*; AMC's *The Walking Dead* and *Breaking Bad*; and ABC's *Pretty Little Liars* (Thielman 2014). By the end of the 2010s, even addressable television had become a reality (Zagorski 2020). To a great extent, these developments enabled campaigns to target communications to specific individuals in ways that mainly direct mail had previously done so and provided campaigns with greater opportunities to deliver customized messages to specific audiences culled using microtargeting and other segmenting techniques.

Changes in campaign finance were also important. The 2000 election was notable for the influx of donations to the Bush campaign. Support for George W. Bush showed up in massive donations, run by pioneers who circumvented individual spending caps by rounding up donations from multiple individuals. This money was poured into advertising, much of it targeted to the evangelical base of the party. Schier (2000) reinforced this point by arguing that specialized interest groups that control considerable financial resources make it vital for candidates to develop microtargeted appeals that cater to these organizations, which are often organized around single issues. The single-issue orientation of these organizations allowed the campaigns to easily design appeals to galvanize the membership of an interest group aligned with their party. The 2000 campaign was the first in which money was mostly raised by the base and spent on the base. This gave Bush the financial resources to comfortably decline public matching funds in the primary elections. This would have boosted each individual donation but imposed overall limits. Since he could rely on private donors to raise money over and above what matching funds would provide, it made sense to avoid the limits by turning down access to funds from the matching scheme.

Despite winning the White House in 2000, by a margin of a single electoral vote and after losing the popular vote to

Democratic Vice President Al Gore and intervention by the U.S. Supreme Court to stop a recount of the decisive votes cast in Florida, Rove believed the Bush campaign underperformed, capturing only 48 percent of the vote compared to Rove's expectation of 50–51 percent (Franke-Ruta 2004). Internal, GOP post-mortem analyses of the 2000 results revealed to Republican National Committee (RNC) Political Director Blaise Hazelwood that union households were turning out at disproportionately higher rates, while Evangelicals were underperforming, putting Republicans at a disadvantage, especially in the final 72 hours of the campaign when union mobilization was strongest. Republicans took action, developing STOMP, the Strategic Task Force to Organize and Mobilize People, to work on the problem. The so-called 72-hour task force deployed predictive analytics, as well as behavioral science approaches, conducting tests of over fifty different organizing methods and doing trial runs in state elections in 2001 (Franke-Ruta 2004) and, later, in trial-by-fire competitive Senate races in Georgia, Minnesota, and South Dakota in 2002 (Nielsen 2012). The 72-hour program was designed to build local volunteer bases willing to work with GOP staffers and party organizations and to combine them with data-based targeting to try to match individual canvassers with voters with whom they shared some affinity, such as neighborhood residence or church affiliation (Nielsen 2012). These efforts paid off handsomely in the 2002 midterm elections when Republicans dispatched more than 1,500 activists and 15,000 volunteers from across the country to sway voters in competitive races (Franke-Ruta 2004). In the end, the share of Republicans voting went up, and the GOP gained seats in Congress for the first time in decades in a midterm election (Franke-Ruta 2004). Four years later, *Time* magazine referred to the 72-hour program as the Republicans' "secret weapon" (Nielsen 2012: 45).

Other campaigns noticed, including Mitt Romney's 2002 campaign for governor of Massachusetts, which turned to GOP consultant Alex Gage and his firm TargetPoint Consulting for expertise in what he called "supersegmentation" at the time (Nielsen 2012). Gage recalled Romney's advisers, many of whom had experience in the corporate world, were reportedly, "flabbergasted when they learned that such techniques, mainstays in corporate America, were not already widespread in politics" (Nielsen 2012: 141).

Lessons learned from tests conducted in 2001 and 2002 informed the George W. Bush re-election campaign in 2004, when strategists doubled down on microtargeting and predictive-modeling approaches (Pierson et al. 2007; Rove 2010). By then, technology had improved, and information collected since 2000 could be used to improve statistical models. Republicans invested heavily in building sophisticated databases of voters, and their Voter Vault platform, which began development in the 1990s but was not used until 2002, contained about 168 million entries by 2004 (Tynan 2004).

Democratic campaigns and organizations, including America Coming Together, realized they had fallen behind and attempted to close the microtargeting gap in the 2004 campaign to elect Massachusetts Senator John Kerry to the presidency. Since 2002, the Democratic Party had relied on two databases—DataMart, the open-source, Democratic equivalent of Voter Vault created by software developer PlusThree that contained about 166 million records of registered voters, and DemZilla, a smaller database used mainly for fundraising and organizing volunteers (Tynan 2004). Their efforts were hampered by a series of problems, however, including uneven data, problems with technical interfaces, and the absence of standardized ways of using new tools (Nielsen 2012: 141). DemZilla and the interface that provided campaigns access to it were ultimately viewed as colossal failures in 2004 (Nielsen 2012).

As Republicans continued to refine and improve their microtargeting capabilities, Democrats eventually started catching up in the 2006 cycle. As Josh Syrjamaki, director of the Minnesota chapter of America Votes, acknowledged, "[i]t's no secret that the other side [Republicans] figured this out a little sooner. They've had four to six years' jump on us on this stuff . . . but we feel like we can start to catch up" (Balz 2006). In 2006, Democratic operatives Harold Ickes and Laura Quinn founded Catalist, a for-profit company to build and maintain a large-scale national database accessible to Democratic campaigns and progressive organizations across the country. After Howard Dean assumed the chairmanship of the Democratic National Committee (DNC) in 2005, he invested $8 million in rebuilding a new national voter file from scratch that contained up to 900 data points appended from a variety of sources (Nielsen 2012). The new venture—VoteBuilder—developed by NGP-VAN, grew quickly and was adopted by thirty state parties and hundreds of campaigns in 2006 (Nielsen 2012). By the time of the 2008 presidential election, VoteBuilder had been strengthened and improved, and both the Democratic primary and general election campaigns featured extensive use of microtargeting and predictive-modeling techniques. In the 2008 cycle, Catalist was the principal repository of Democratic data and acted "as the conductor for a data-driven symphony of more than 90 liberal groups, like the Service Employees Union—and the DNC—and the Obama campaign" (Ambinder 2009). Investments in building these databases and platforms continued once Barack Obama was elected and transferred much of his data analytics machinery to the DNC as a special project titled "Organizing for America" (Nielsen 2012).

Reliance on microtargeting, analytics, and predictive modeling has been a central feature of presidential campaigns on both sides of the political aisle ever since. On the Republican side, the Trump campaign invested heavily in microtargeting to reach specific voters in 2016, especially on digital platforms like Google, Snapchat, Twitter, Facebook, and YouTube, and famously hired the now-defunct Cambridge Analytica for assistance. The firm specialized in "psychographic" targeting that integrates insights about individuals' personalities into its models and claimed to possess over 5,000 data points on each of the 200 million voters in the United States that could be used to build accurate psychological profiles and to develop effective messaging for targeted individuals (Dehay 2016). Cambridge Analytica, which initially worked for Ted Cruz in the 2016 GOP primary campaign until he dropped out, bragged about its blueprint for the Trump victory in 2018, noting that "intensive survey research, data modeling and performance-optimising algorithms were used to target 10,000 different ads viewed billions of times to different audiences in the months leading up to the election" (Lewis and Hilder 2018). Extensive use of analytics and predictive modeling also featured prominently in Hillary Clinton's campaign for the White House in 2016. Currently, Democrats continue to use VoterBuilder while Republicans have transitioned to a new system—Data Trust—and several, nonpartisan firms offer data on registered voters, including NationBuilder, Aristotle, eMerges, and Labels and Lists. Karl Rove, who views the partisan battle for data supremacy as a sort of modern arms race, claims Republicans reclaimed dominance in 2016 and argues, "Data Trust was a big reason why Donald Trump won the 2016 election," (Rove 2019). By contrast, Rove (2019) noted, "Hillary Clinton. . . complained. . . she inherited 'nothing from the Democratic Party. . . . Its data was mediocre to poor, nonexistent, wrong," in part, Rove claimed, because the 2012 Obama campaign refused to turn over much of its data and digital tools to the Democratic National Committee after the election. Republicans continued to grow their data edge in the 2018 cycle, Rove (2019) observed, but he concedes any "data supremacy" the GOP might enjoy is unlikely to go unchallenged. The political data arms race continued full-tilt in the 2020 cycle (Kozlowski 2019).

MICROTARGETING AND BASE MAXIMIZATION

The development, adoption, and proliferation of microtargeting, predictive modeling, and analytics techniques in political campaigns that took place in the early 2000s had a profound impact on campaign strategy. Specifically, it facilitated and accelerated the shift in the strategic prioritization of base maximization and base mobilization in presidential campaigns that I observed over the course of the past few decades. As Chuck Todd and Carrie Dann (2017) argue, "candidates and lawmakers have been increasingly incentivized—and enabled by Big Data—to cater to their bases to the exclusion of other voters." But why? After all, Hillygus and Shields (2008) have convincingly argued that microtargeting can be—and has been—used effectively to persuade voters in elections. The authors demonstrate that campaigns use microtargeting to narrowcast specific messages—like wedge issues—to cross-pressured voters sympathetic to their candidate's position on certain issues without risking the backlash that could be associated with broader telecasting of these messages. I do not take issue with the claim that microtargeting can be deployed to identify and target swing or persuadable voters, nor am I arguing that political campaigns have abandoned outreach to these voters entirely. In fact, it is conceivable—and consistent with evidence summarized in subsequent chapters—that campaigns are targeting both base partisans and swing voters at higher rates. Rather, I argue that microtargeting lends itself more easily to mobilization than to persuasion efforts and that, partly as a result, presidential campaigns' attention to base partisans has grown gradually in recent decades, especially relative to the rate at which persuadable voters have been targeted by these campaigns. Todd and Dann (2017) concur, noting, "Big Data— a combination of massive technological power and endlessly detailed voter information—now allows campaigns to pinpoint their most likely supporters. These tools make mobilizing supporters easier, faster and far less expensive than persuading their neighbors." "[T]hanks to the advent of micro-targeting," the authors continue, "campaign consultants realized that the easiest way to win wasn't to persuade the folks in the middle at all. Instead, data could be used to activate every possible base voter and build a partisan firewall" (Todd and Dann 2017). In sum, the focus on the base has likely accelerated with the development of predictive-modeling and microtargeting techniques described earlier in the chapter.

This view is echoed by Eitan Hersh (2015: 22) who observes, "unlike public records of partisanship and race, which, when they are available, are highly predictive of political support, there are essentially no records available to campaigns that are consistently predictive of persuadablity. Persuadability is a psychological predisposition that campaigns have no good way to estimate." Hersh (2015) replicates the kinds of strategies that campaigns use to use to determine which voters should receive persuasion appeals and connects these voters with survey data to show that typical voters targeted for persuasion do not resemble the kinds of voters that survey researchers would classify as persuadable. On the basis of these analyses, Hersh (2015: 22) concludes that "campaigns cannot effectively target persuadable voters. As a result, persuasion efforts in direct contacting strategies are less efficient than mobilization efforts. The voters who are most ripe for persuasion cannot be pinpointed for individual-level contact."

Campaigns are not oblivious to this. Nor is the notion that persuasion is difficult new to them. Research by social scientists dating back to the 1940s has consistently demonstrated that voter preferences are relatively stable (Lazarsfeld, Berelson, and Gaudet 1944; Zaller 1992) and, while not completely impervious (Gerber et al. 2011; Erikson and Wlezien 2012; Panagopoulos 2009a; Erikson, Panagopoulos, and Wlezien 2010), are generally highly resistant to change (Kalla and Broockman 2018). This is in part because individuals tend to consume, retain, and expose themselves to information selectively, favoring views that reinforce their existing predispositions and avoiding contradictory information (Zaller 1992). Efforts designed to detect evidence of persuasion routinely fail to do so (Kalla and Broockman 2018). The use of wedge issues, in particular, has become far riskier in an environment in which stealth, below-the-radar wedge issue campaigns have the potential to become front-page news or featured prominently in national and mass media outlets. None of this should be interpreted to imply that no one is ever persuaded by any information, but rather that persuasion is a challenging and unreliable enterprise. As Gardner (2009: 86) notes, "[i]t is important to be clear here. The social science literature does not say—and I do not wish to be understood as characterizing it to say—that people are never persuaded, whether in the ideal sense or in some other lesser sense by political information and arguments, whether provided by candidates, officials, voters, or other political actors. The literature does, however, make an extremely powerful case that people almost never change their beliefs and opinions to any significant degree *during campaigns*" (emphasis in original). Even when persuasive communications do manage to nudge voters' views successfully, their effects dissipate quickly, typically within a matter of days (Gerber et al. 2011).

By contrast, social and behavioral scientists have conducted hundreds of randomized interventions in real-world settings over the past two decades or so that have produced numerous insights about how to mobilize voters effectively (Green and

Gerber 2012; Issenberg 2012). Among the most robust findings is that door-to-door canvassing is one of the most effective tactics available (Green and Gerber 2012; Gerber and Green 2000). Personalized appeals (Green and Gerber 2012; Nielsen 2012), volunteer phone calls, and messages that leverage social pressure (Gerber, Green, and Larimer 2008, 2010; Condon, Larimer and Panagopoulos 2016; Panagopoulos, Larimer and Condon 2014; Panagopoulos 2014; Panagopoulos 2013) or gratitude expression (Panagopoulos 2011) also appear to stimulate voting effectively. An exhaustive review of this burgeoning literature is beyond the scope of the current study, but these examples highlight the basic point: Campaigns increasingly have access to an abundance of evidence about the kinds of tactics that effectively bring voters to the polls, while guidance about effective persuasion strategies remain elusive. Coupled with the capacity to scale these efforts offered by microtargeting, these insights have revolutionized how contemporary political campaigns approach voter contact and mobilization in elections (Issenberg 2012; Nielsen 2012; Green and Gerber 2012).

To be fair, while some observers have lauded the potential of microtargeted campaigns to increase turnout (Schier 2000), others have raised concerns about the potential deterioration of personal privacy (Cohen 2000). For example, in 2013, testimony in the U.S. Senate revealed that some companies had lists of the names of survivors of rape and sexual assault that could be purchased for commercial purposes at the price of $0.79 per name (Senate Committee on Commerce, Science, and Transportation, December 18, 2013). Scholars have also considered the implications for the quality of democratic deliberation. As Gardner (2009: 69) has argued, "[s]urely such a system is unlikely to produce mass raiding by persuasion of each party's membership by the other. A much more likely result is that such a system of mass organizational speech will quickly degenerate into a shouting match directed at a small minority of voters." These debates took center stage in 2018 when it was revealed that Cambridge Analytica had harvested personal data from 70 million Americans' Facebook profiles without their consent during the 2016 presidential race and used it for political targeting purposes (Davies 2015). Data breaches involving the DNC and the Democratic Congressional Campaign Committee were also reported in 2016 (Yourish 2018). Increasingly, data vendors have come under fire for the vast and detailed information they collect, as well as for security concerns. Cybersecurity researcher Chris Vickery, who discovered the unprotected files of 198 million Americans compiled by GOP data firm Deep Root Analytics in a routine scan of the Internet in 2017, claimed he, " . . . could give you the home address of every person the RNC believes voted for Trump," (Fung, Timberg and Gold 2017). Jeffrey Chester, executive director of the Center for Digital Democracy, sounded the alarm, noting, "[t]hese political data firms might as well be working for the Russians," (Fung, Timberg and Gold 2017). Such concerns about access to political data and security remain potent.

Targeted outreach and communications may also not be silver bullets for political campaigns. Hersh (2015) cautions that predictive models can be inaccurate or misleading, skewing campaigns' perceptions of voters and their attitudinal or behavioral propensities. There is also the possibility that voters are savvy enough to recognize and reject targeted appeals, or even to penalize candidates who traffic in microtargeting. An intriguing study by Hersh and Schaffner (2013) finds that voters rarely prefer targeted pandering to general messages and that "mistargeted" voters penalize candidates enough to erase the positive returns to targeting. The authors conclude that while targeting may theoretically allow candidates to quietly promise particularistic benefits to narrow audiences, thereby altering the nature of political representation, but voters seem to prefer being solicited based on broad principles and collective benefits (Hersh and Schaffner 2013).

These cautionary tales and high-profile scandals underscore potent concerns about microtargeting practices, but the technology is likely to remain a mainstay of political campaigns for the foreseeable future.

THE ELUSIVE

PERSUADABLE VOTER

Karl [Rove] does not believe there's a true "middle."
—GEORGE W. BUSH QUOTED IN KORNBLUT 2004

COUNTLESS CHOICES ARE MADE OVER the course of a political campaign as operatives seek to devise effective strategies, adapt to changing circumstances, and react to their opponents and other developments. Among the most fundamental—and potentially consequential—decisions campaigns must make, however, is to determine the optimal balance between targeting likely supporters and focusing on undecided or persuadable voters in their quest for victory. To put it another way, campaigns must decide whether to fish where the fish are or to cast a wide net. Ideally, campaigns would do both, but resources like time, money, and attention are not unlimited, and efficient allocation of available resources can be decisive.

In Chapter 2, I summarized developments in the growth of microtargeting and described its capacity to help campaigns decipher which voters to target. I also argued that persuasion is notoriously difficult for campaigns to achieve and that mobilizing predisposed supporters may be a more promising avenue. The dominant view, as summarized by Berelson, Lazarsfeld, and McPhee (1954: 248), is that a campaign "crystallizes and reinforces more than it converts." Accordingly, as McClurg and Habel (2011: 212) note, campaigns "are less about persuading

Bases Loaded. Costas Panagopoulos, Oxford University Press (2021). © Oxford University Press.
DOI: 10.1093/oso/9780197533062.001.0001.

independents and opponents and more about rekindling dormant loyalties and gathering support on Election Day." Stated differently, "campaigns tend to preach to a chorus of partisans who are more likely to say 'Hallelujah' than they are to consider the merits of the sermon" (McClurg and Habel 2011: 213).

Nevertheless, Hillygus and Shields (2008) have shown that persuadable voters are plentiful, comprising, depending on how they are defined, as much as two-thirds of all voters and that presidential campaigns do engage in persuasion efforts targeting these voters in elections. In contemplating strategic targeting, one calculation operatives must consider relates to the relative sizes of these two segments of the voting population—the base versus persuadable voters. In some cases, campaigns may have no choice but to engage in base expansion—convincing voters on the fence or converting out-partisans to support their candidate—because the sizes of their respective bases is insufficient to win, but in other circumstances, focusing on maximizing base participation may be enough.

It is reasonable to consider just how large the respective pools of base and persuadable voters are in contemporary elections and how the compositions of these segments of the voting population have changed in recent cycles. One complication, however, is that there is not necessarily a consensus about how to define persuadable voters (Mayer 2007), and analytic choices about classification schemes can have a significant impact on the outcomes of these estimations. Resolving these concerns is beyond the scope of this book, but I examine a series of indicators to gauge whether any patterns become apparent. Overall, the analyses presented in this chapter suggest that the number of voters available for persuasion nationally, while not inconsequential, has been shrinking over time, thus limiting campaigns' opportunities to convert voters. At the same time, the party bases appear to be growing and the impact of partisan identification on vote choice has risen sharply. These findings are broadly consistent with observations several other analysts have offered in recent years (Abramowitz 2011; McClurg and Habel 2011), and these circumstances have reconfigured the context in which presidential campaigns must operate and make strategic choices.

The empirical analyses presented in this chapter are based on data from the American National Election Studies Time Series Cumulative Data File (better known as ANES). Analyses are conducted on full samples and weighted (details available upon request).

PARTISANSHIP OVER TIME

I begin by examining patterns in partisan identification in presidential election cycles between 1956 and 2016. The ANES asks respondents to place themselves on a 7-point scale that ranges from strong Democrat at one end to strong Republican on the other. Respondents can also identify as "weak" partisans or as independents, who are subsequently asked whether they "lean" more toward one party or the other (leaners). Those who indicate they lean toward neither party are typically viewed as "pure" or "true" independents.

Partisanship in the American electorate has been studied extensively for decades using these data. One recent study shows the percentage of voters who have relatively weak partisan beliefs have comprised a majority of the electorate consistently over the past sixty years (McClurg and Habel 2011). This group is roughly twice the size of the most committed voter, the strong identifiers, and they outnumber non-identifiers (true independents and apolitical voters) by nearly six to one (McClurg and Habel 2011: 215). In this analysis, the authors conclude that these weak partisans are prime targets for campaigns because, while they have an affinity for one party or another, they also harbor more ambivalence toward the parties than do strong partisans". . . . [I]t is among these 'peripheral partisans' where campaigns can get the most 'bang for their buck'" (McClurg and Habel 2011: 215).

In my view, peripheral voters require at least some level of persuasion, given their weak partisan predispositions. Accordingly, a more measured approach might be to compare the relative sizes of the most committed voters (strong partisans)—the base—with the least committed to party (pure independents), who could be viewed most defensibly as persuadable. Such an analysis, presented in Figure 3.1, shows strong partisans have consistently outnumbered pure independents in the electorate over the past six decades. On average, the share

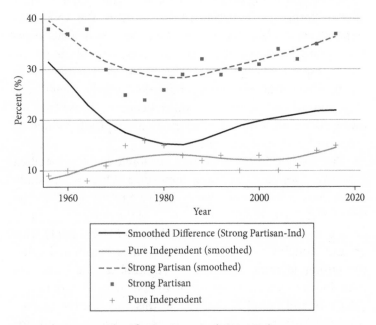

FIGURE 3.1 Partisan Identification Intensity (1956–2016) *Source*: Compiled by author from ANES Time Series Cumulative File (full samples, weighted).

of the most committed partisans has been two-to-three times the size of the pool of the most detached (in terms of partisan affiliation) Americans over this period. Moreover, the solid line, which represents a Lowess-smoothed version of the difference between the shares of strong partisans versus pure independents, reveals that the former has been on the rise consistently since the early 1980s, relative to the latter, implying the growth in the number of strong partisans has been increasingly outpacing shifts in the share of pure independents. This initial evidence suggests the prospects for persuasion have been on the decline, especially in recent cycles, while the partisan bases—those voters most ripe for mobilization—have been growing.

CROSS-PRESSURED PARTISANS OVER TIME

Of course this is not the only way to conceptualize and classify persuadable voters. An alternative approach is offered by Hillygus and Shields (2008) in their seminal book on these voters. The authors view persuadable voters as cross-pressured partisans, that is, these voters disagree with their party's policy position on at least one issue (Hillygus and Shields 2008). Cross-pressured partisans are more and more likely to defect as the number of issues on which they disagree with their party increases (Repass 1971). Hillygus and Shields (2008) trace the extent of policy incongruence over time by examining the percentage of partisans between 1972 and 2004 who report disagreement with their affiliated party on at least one issue and find similar proportions of such partisans over this period. As an alternative measure of cross-pressure, Hillygus and Shields (2008: 70) also examine the percentages of people who report disliking something about their preferred political party from an open-ended question included on the ANES. Here too, the authors find substantial stability in responses with around half of respondents volunteering something they dislike about the party to which they belong.

Overall, Hillygus and Shields (2008) report more stability than change in the number of persuadable voters over the period they examine, but they concede there is at least some evidence of decline. "Looking carefully at the patterns over time," they note, "we see a hint of a decline in policy incongruence between 1992 and 2004" (Hillygus and Shields 2008: 70). Focusing on levels of policy incongruence on specific issues over time, again the authors observe "a small decline in the prevalence of some issues in recent years," but they ultimately conclude, "the clearest pattern is one of overall stability" (Hillygus and Shields 2008: 71). Stronger evidence of declining cross-pressures in the electorate is presented by Lawrence (2001) in his analysis of the period 1952 to 1996. Lawrence (2001) examines issue- and candidate-oriented cross-pressures in these election cycles, as measured by likes and dislikes of the parties and candidates expressed in open-ended questions included on the ANES, and concludes that, despite increasing between the 1950s and 1970s, cross-pressures of both types began to decline starting in the 1970s.

To get a better sense of more recent developments, Figure 3.2 extends the Hillygus and Shields (2008) series of partisans cross-pressured on at least one issue by two election cycles (2008 and 2012).[1] Consistent with estimates reported in Hillygus and Shields (2008), replication reveals that nearly all partisans are cross-pressured. On average, 82 percent of partisans over this period are cross-pressured on at least one issue, and policy incongruence even exceeds 90 percent in two of the eleven presidential cycles examined. Nevertheless, the Lowess-smoothed line implies the percentage of cross-pressured partisans, which had been growing since early 1970s, began to decline starting in the mid-to-late 1990s. In the four most recent cycles included in the analysis (2000–2012), the decline has been quite pronounced, and levels of policy incongruence, while still relatively

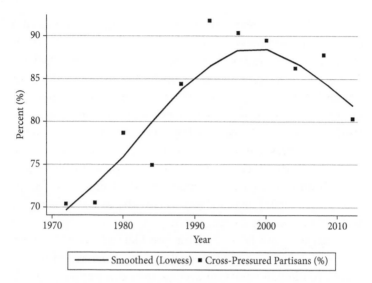

FIGURE 3.2 Cross-Pressured Partisans Over Time (1972–2012)
Source: Endres 2016.

high, appear to be reverting back to levels typically observed in the 1970s and 1980s.

In tandem with the other evidence just summarized, the inclusion of two additional presidential election cycles suggests the "hint of decline" observed by Hillygus and Shields (2008) using data through 2004 has, in fact, persisted. Policy incongruence now appears to be reliably retrenching in the electorate, a pattern that is consistent with the argument that the number of persuadable voters is declining.

SWING VOTERS OVER TIME

Mayer (2007) proposes yet another alternative way to conceptualize swing voters in presidential elections. The author exploits differences in how favorably or unfavorably ANES respondents reported feeling about the major-party presidential candidates using feeling thermometers that ranged from 0 to 100 as a measure of "swingness" or convertability. Mayer (2007) argues these favorability ratings represent a meaningful summary indicator of how respondents evaluate specific individuals or groups that are highly correlated with other important political variables like voting behavior and ideological self-identification. He develops a scale constructed by subtracting the rating for the Democratic presidential candidate from that of the Republican nominee, so that higher scale scores indicate relatively higher Republican favorability compared with the Democratic candidate. Mayer (2007) classified any voter with a score between –15 and +15 inclusive as a swing voter.

Analyzing available data for presidential cycles between 1972 and 2004, the author estimated that 23 percent of major-party presidential voters on average over this period could be considered swing voters using this criterion (Mayer 2007). He observed some variation across cycles but did not focus much on developments over time. A closer look at Mayer's (2007) estimates of swing voters in these cycles over time suggests the share of such voters had declined sharply over this period. I replicated these analyses for these cycles (and found results nearly identical to those reported in Mayer 2007) and extended the series through the 2016 election.

The complete series, displayed in Figure 3.3, makes evident the declining number of swing voters in presidential elections over this period. The trend has not abated since 2004, when Mayer's (2007) analysis concluded. In fact, the 2012 and 2016 cycles registered the two lowest levels of swing voters (9 and 8 percent respectively) recorded since 1972. Overall, the share of swing voters in presidential elections over this period has declined by about 1.7 percentage points on average per cycle (standard error = .38, p = .001, two-tailed). Comparing rates of change before and since the 2000 cycle reveals the share of swing voters had been declining before 2000 but at a relatively modest (and statistically insignificant) rate of about 1.35 percentage

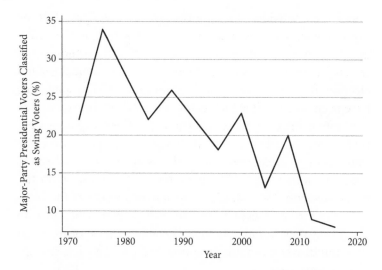

FIGURE 3.3 Major-Party Presidential Voters Classified as Swing Voters (1972–2016) *Source*: 1972–2004: Mayer (2007); 2008–2016: Compiled by author from ANES Time Series Cumulative File.

points per cycle on average (standard error = .90, *p* = .19, two-tailed). By contrast, the average rate of decline in the percentage of swing voters since 2000 is more than double, falling by 3.4 percentage points on average per cycle during the last five presidential elections (standard error = 1.43, *p* = .098, two-tailed).

Using Mayer's (2007) alternative method to operationalize and estimate the number of swing voters in elections tells a story similar to the one that emerged earlier: The number of swing, persuadable, or convertible voters in presidential elections is relatively scarce, and these voters are becoming increasingly elusive.

TIMING OF VOTING DECISIONS OVER TIME

Another alternative way to think about persuadability is to consider what people say about the timing of their voting decisions.

The ANES provides an opportunity to investigate this by exploiting an item designed to get some traction on the points at which respondents report making up their minds about which candidate they would support in the presidential general election. In every presidential election since 1956, respondents have been asked, "How long before the election did you decide you were going to vote the way you did?" Their responses were then coded, based on key moments of the campaign timeline, into one of six categories: (1) they knew all along; (2) when the candidate announced; (3) during the conventions; (4) in the post-convention period; (5) in the last two weeks of the campaign; and (6) on Election Day.[2] In theory, voters who knew all along how they would vote in the general election or made up their minds when candidates announced are likely less susceptible to persuasion.

Figure 3.4 presents the results of a weighted multinomial logit analysis (details available upon request) to generate predicted probabilities of respondents reporting to make up their minds during respective phases of the campaign over time. The evidence makes several points clear. First, most people report knowing all along which candidate they would support on Election Day. This is unsurprising given the outsized—and strengthening—role that partisanship plays in determining vote choice in presidential elections (Abramowitz 2011). What is striking, however, is the fact that voters over the period examined are more and more likely to report knowing all along which candidate they would vote for or to decide when the candidates announced. In the most recent cycles, the likelihood that voters decide during this early stage of the election exceeds 50 percent. Compare that with the 1950s and 1960s, when the likelihood of deciding so early was 35–40 percent. By contrast, the likelihood of deciding during the conventions or in the post-convention period has declined precipitously, while the prospects for decision-making during the last two weeks of the campaign or on Election Day are virtually unchanged over the past six decades.

To what extent is partisan intensity driving the patterns detected in Figure 3.4? To investigate this question, I examined the timing of voting decisions by partisan subgroups. The results of the analyses are presented in Figure 3.5. Visual inspection of the evidence reveals the growth in knowing all along which candidates voters would support appears to be driven by voters with the strongest partisan ties (strong partisans). The likelihood of deciding in the next phase of the campaign—when candidates announce—is higher for all partisan subgroups, including, interestingly, for pure independents who presumably have few partisan connections. Pure independents are also most likely (and increasingly so over this period) to make up their minds during the last two weeks of the campaign compared with voters in the other partisan subgroups, but these voters overall in recent cycles are more likely to know all along

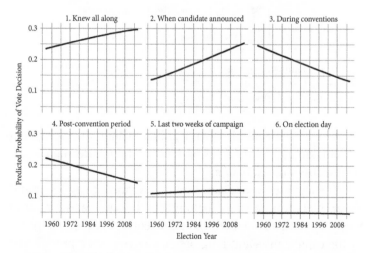

FIGURE 3.4 Timing of Voting Decisions (1956–2016) *Source*: Compiled by author from ANES Cumulative File (full samples, weighted). Lines represent linear trends.

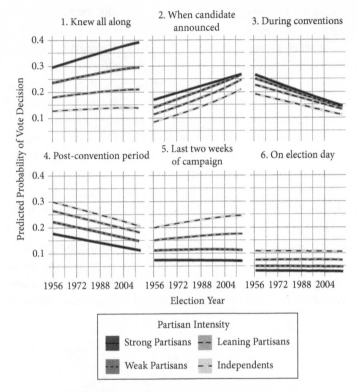

FIGURE 3.5 Timing of Voting Decisions by Partisan Subgroups (1956–2016) *Source*: Compiled by author from ANES Time Series Cumulative File (full samples, weighted). Lines represent linear trends.

or make up their minds when candidates announce compared with making up their minds on Election Day or during the last two weeks of the campaign.

The analyses of decision timing described imply fewer and fewer voters are undecided for long after the candidates announce their intentions. Long before the conventions or the final phase of the campaigns—and long before contemporary presidential campaigns begin in earnest—most voters, including most persuadable voters (in this case, defined as pure independents), have made up their minds about who they will support on Election Day. I contend this limits campaign's capacity to influence their decisions, implying campaigns may be most impactful by focusing on identifying supporters and pouring their energy into mobilizing them to vote on Election Day.

PARTY VOTING: 1956—2016

In thinking about opportunities for strategic mobilization or persuasion by campaigns, one other aspect of voting behavior may be relevant: party voting. That is, how many partisans ultimately choose their party's presidential nominee on Election Day—and how has this changed over the past sixty years. Once again, I turn to data collected by the ANES to examine these questions. Figure 3.6 displays the share of

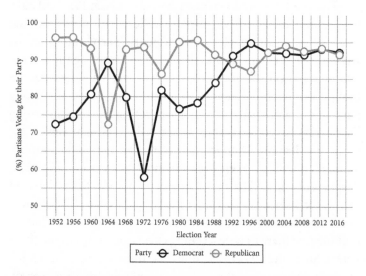

FIGURE 3.6 Party Vote Rates by Party (1956–2016) *Source*: Compiled by author from ANES Time Series Cumulative File (full samples, weighted).

partisans who report voting for their party's presidential candidate on Election Day by voters' partisan affiliations. The data shows that—for both Democrats and Republicans—the lion's share of voters report voting for their party's nominee. This is especially true of Republican identifiers consistently throughout this period, but Democrats have caught up in recent elections. In fact, over 90 percent of Democrats report supporting the Democratic presidential nominee in every election cycle since 1992. In thirteen of the sixteen election cycles examined—including the last five elections—more than 90 percent of Republicans indicated they voted for the GOP contender. Strikingly, since the 2000 election, for the first time in the past six decades, more than 90 percent of partisans on both sides of the aisle have reported voting for their respective party's candidate on Election Day. With so few partisans defecting in presidential contests, the opportunities for persuasion appear slim.

Figure 3.7 breaks down party voting between 1956 and 2016 by partisan subgroups to explore differences across varying levels of intensity of party attachments. Party voting across strength of attachment has fluctuated—often significantly—over this period. As expected, however, party voting rates are highest on average across these presidential cycles for strong partisans in both major parties. Party voting rates among strong Democrats have grown sharply since the 1980s, as well as for weak and leaning Democrats. Voting for the GOP nominee among Republican voters has been more stable over this period; despite a dip in 1992—when 15 percent of Republicans defected to vote for someone other than President George H. W. Bush— over 90 percent of strong Republicans have voted for their party's nominee, so there may be a ceiling effect operating among these voters. Since the 1992 cycle, however, there has been an uptick in party voting among weak and leaning Republicans overall, but a bit of a decline among weak Republicans in the three most

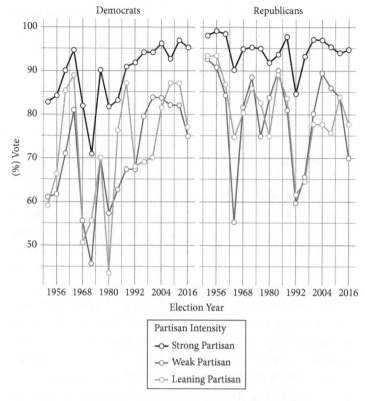

FIGURE 3.7 Party Vote Rates by Partisan Subgroups (1956–2016)
Source: Compiled by author from ANES Time Series Cumulative File (full samples, weighted).

recent cycles. Party voting among weak and leaning Republicans appears to have declined somewhat since high points in 1956 and 1960, but it still has exceeded 70 percent of voters in both groups in the past five cycles. Overall, even among partisan leaners, party voting has been quite high, exceeding 75 percent on average over this period. On the whole, these trends are consistent with patterns identified by other scholars, including Abramowitz (2015), who concludes party loyalty and straight-ticket voting have reached record levels in recent years. In addition, the impact of partisan identification on vote choice strengthens over the course of the campaign as preferences crystallize (Erikson, Panagopoulos, and Wlezien 2010).

CONCLUSION

Taken together, the bulk of the evidence presented in this chapter suggests the opportunities campaigns have for persuasion may be limited. It is also likely they are diminishing over time as fewer voters identify as pure independents or can be classified as swing voters, as policy incongruence is declining, as a growing number of voters are making up their minds about which presidential candidates to support even before the campaigns begin, and as party defection rates across the board are low and shrinking. Faced with these developments—an ever-decreasing pool of persuadable voters to target and bases that are growing—it is reasonable to expect that campaigns would shift gears in recent election cycles to focus more on mobilization, or maximizing participation among base supporters, relative to pouring their energy into the incredible difficult task of persuading voters to support their candidates—and then mobilizing them to vote too. In the next chapter, I analyze voter contact patterns in election cycles since 1956 to provide a glimpse into presidential campaigns' strategic priorities over this period.

SWITCHING GEARS

Changing Voter Contact Strategies in Presidential Elections

> We shouldn't be putting 80 percent of our resources into persuasion and 20 percent into base motivation, which is basically what had been happening up until that point.
>
> —MATTHEW DOWD, *Chief Campaign Strategist Bush-Cheney 2004 (Frontline 2005)*

> Why try to change the mind of one skeptic . . . when in the same amount of time you could make sure five core supporters commit to go to the polls?
>
> —TODD AND DANN (2017)

FOR DECADES, POLITICAL SCIENTISTS HAVE heralded the theory that parties that capture the median voter in elections are victorious (Downs 1957). This so-called median voter theorem has cultivated the lore that campaigns should converge at the political center, but that may be a flawed interpretation. As Campbell (2016: 207) warns, contrary to the median voter theorem and the conventional wisdom of centrism that has developed around it, it may not be in the parties' electoral self-interests to converge at the center of the ideological spectrum. Put simply: "Single-minded centrism is not politically smart" (Campbell 2016: 207). Parties should not ignore centrist voters but should not cater to them either (Campbell 2016: 207).

Bases Loaded. Costas Panagopoulos, Oxford University Press (2021). © Oxford University Press.
DOI: 10.1093/oso/9780197533062.001.0001.

Although parties may be tempted to take the support of their bases for granted, and decide not to expend precious resources on cultivating these votes, strong support from the ideological base is a "necessary component to any majority coalition" (Campbell 2016: 213). Kessel (1992) puts it bluntly: If a campaign fails to capture its base, it will fail completely. Votes from the base are not a sure thing (Campbell 2016: 215), however, and political campaigns must be deliberate in prioritizing them, often at the cost of other targets.

Perhaps the most fundamental and potentially consequential decision political campaigns typically face is how to balance appealing to their bases and to centrist, swing, or persuadable voters. One rationale asserts such choices are not necessarily zero sum. Targeting the base can reverberate with other voters. This was clearly a perspective George W. Bush's campaign team had internalized. One adviser, quoted in Kornblut (2004), noted Karl Rove believed everyone was a leaner and that, "leaners are affected by the actions of the base, much like an earthquake. If the base is excited, the closer you are to the epicenter, you're going to have a pretty strong shock." Burton, Miller, and Shea (2015: 102) echo this view, noting, "energizing the base increases the number of votes among natural supporters while at the same time gathering up a quantity of centrists who feel the effects of base enthusiasm." But such strategic decisions can also create dilemmas for campaigns because appeals to the center may cost votes in the base and vice versa (Campbell 2016). Movement in either direction is risky and may not be cost free, but Campbell (2016: 218) observes, "[n]either party can reach the median voter unless it has satisfied its ideological base."

Throughout this book, I have advanced the claim that political campaigns in recent cycles have turned their attention disproportionately to voters in their respective partisan bases relative to persuadable or swing voters. I argue this represents a shift in the direction of a base maximization strategy, whereby campaigns focus on mobilizing core supporters, as opposed to base expansion, or an effort to convince voters to make up their minds or to defect across the partisan aisle, and I investigate this in the context of presidential elections over the past six decades, when other fundamental changes to the sociopolitical landscape have been underway. But how would we document such a shift? Direct, empirical evidence on this score is not so easy to come by. In the first place, presidential campaigns are constantly in flux, and consistent, reliable records or measures of campaign strategy are unavailable over the course of several election cycles.

In this chapter, I attempt to track presidential campaigns' strategic priorities indirectly by exploiting observational data on self-reported voter contact by political campaigns collected by the American National Election Studies since 1956. These patterns will enable me to trace meaningful changes to determine whether campaigns have targeted different kinds of voters over time, and whether there is support in the evidence for the corollary claim I have advanced that the 2000 election represents a turning point in these processes. Anecdotal accounts of this shift in strategy are consistent with existing scholarship (Panagopoulos and Wielhouwer 2008; Francia and Panagopoulos 2009; Beck and Heidemann 2014; Wielhouwer 1995) that finds a sharp overall increase in contacting voters starting with the 2000 election and continuing in subsequent cycles, but I argue the intensified mobilization has been unevenly distributed and concentrated among base partisans relative to persuadable or independent voters.

CAMPAIGN CONTACT: A MICRO-LEVEL ANALYSIS

Insights about campaign strategy are typically inferred from empirical evidence about voter contact in election cycles. A common source for examining voter contact is the American National Election Studies (ANES). I use the ANES Time Series

Cumulative File to examine contacting activity over the past few decades. The analyses are restricted to presidential election years only. Questions about voter contact in presidential election years first appeared on the ANES in 1956, providing us with six decades of survey data from sixteen presidential election cycles (1956–2016) for analysis.

My analyses focus on the following ANES question (with only slight variations in some years): "The political parties try to talk to as many people as they can to get them to vote for their candidate(s). Did anyone from one of the political parties call you up or come around and talk to you about the campaign? If yes, which party was that?" I acknowledge certain limitations to this measure of campaign contact. Some analysts contend recollections about party contact may be inaccurate. When other ANES questions relying on respondent recall have been subjected to external validation, these memories have been broadly validated. Therefore I take this variable at face value as a measure of contact rates. Even if the core constituents of a party are simply more likely to remember being contacted, rather than actually being contacted more often, this bias is likely to be constant over different election cycles and would not confound inferences about changes over time (McDonald 2003).[1]

Additionally, I acknowledge that respondents who report being contacted by a campaign are not probed about whether it was the presidential campaign or perhaps a statewide, congressional, or local campaign organization. There is also no indication of the timing or frequency of campaign contact. As such, there is no way to differentiate whether contact was experienced during the primary or general elections, for example, and, presumably, at least some portion of reported contact was intraparty, occurring during presidential primary campaigns. Despite these, and potentially other, limitations, the ANES measure of voter contact is commonly used and consistently available for several decades (Beck and Heidemann 2014;

Francia and Panagopoulos 2009; Panagopoulos and Wielhouwer 2008; Wielhouwer 1995; Rosenstone and Hansen 1993).

Furthermore, I recognize that if self-reported party contact increases among partisans but not independents, this could reflect changes in campaign targeting, but it could also result from some individuals finding such contacts more memorable. Similarly, if a party simply becomes better at contacting voters, perhaps because of technological advances or increasing budgets, and the number of independent voters also declines over time, then statistical correlations would still show that the party in question is contacting its partisans more over time even if there had not been a change in targeting strategies. This possibility, and other similar plausible scenarios regarding changes in the partisan makeup of the electorate, suggests the empirical evidence presented in this chapter is only one part of the puzzle. Still, these concerns can be at least somewhat assuaged by illustrating that this evidence emerges consistently under a variety of different statistical model specifications.

I begin by displaying overall contact rates broken down by partisan identification. For this commonly used measure, respondents are asked a pair of questions that can be used to construct a 7-point scale, ranging from strong Democrat (1), through independent (4), to strong Republican (7). Below I collapse (or fold) this scale to focus on partisan intensity; that is, strong Democrats are coded with strong Republicans as strong partisans (3), and so on, down to pure independents, who are coded as zero.

Figure 4.1 shows the proportion of respondents in each subgroup (or combined) who report being contacted by either the Democrats or the Republicans or both in each presidential cycle included in my analysis.[2] Taken as a whole, the evidence reveals voters across the partisan spectrum report being contacted at increasingly higher rates over the course of the six decades examined. While about one-quarter to one-fifth of

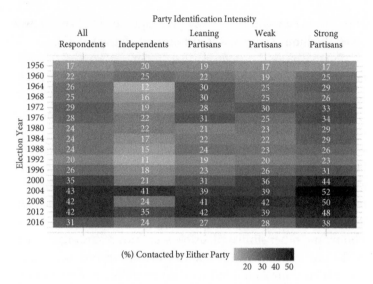

Party Identification Intensity

Election Year	All Respondents	Independents	Leaning Partisans	Weak Partisans	Strong Partisans
1956	17	20	19	17	17
1960	22	25	22	19	25
1964	26	12	30	25	29
1968	25	16	30	25	26
1972	29	19	28	30	33
1976	28	22	31	25	34
1980	24	22	21	23	29
1984	24	17	22	22	29
1988	24	15	24	23	26
1992	20	11	19	20	23
1996	26	18	23	26	31
2000	35	21	31	36	44
2004	43	41	39	39	52
2008	42	24	41	42	50
2012	42	35	42	39	48
2016	31	24	27	28	38

(%) Contacted by Either Party

20 30 40 50

FIGURE 4.1 Voter Contact by Either Party Overall and by Partisan Intensity (1956–2016) *Source*: Compiled by author from ANES Time Series Cumulative File (full samples, weighted).

voters overall report being contacted by one party or the other in elections in the 1950s and 1960s, more than one-in-three voters report contact by either party in elections since 2000. The biggest jump in overall contact rates occurs between the 1996 and 2000 elections. In fact, the 9 percentage-point bump in overall contact observed in 2000 among all respondents can be decomposed into an increase of 13 percentage points on average for strong partisans, more than four times as large as the 3 percentage-point increase in contact experienced by pure independents over these two cycles. Not only was there an important change in 2000, but this shift was experienced more strongly by the base. This pattern was repeated in 2004, when overall contact jumped by another 8 percentage points, with a noticeable spike in reported contact by pure independents that reverted in 2008.

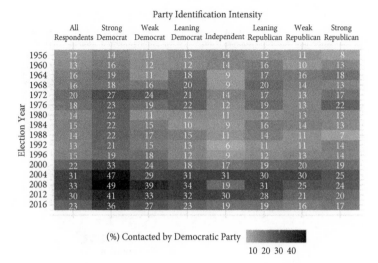

Party Identification Intensity

Election Year	All Respondents	Strong Democrat	Weak Democrat	Leaning Democrat	Independent	Leaning Republican	Weak Republican	Strong Republican
1956	12	14	11	13	14	12	11	8
1960	13	16	12	12	14	16	10	13
1964	16	19	11	18	9	17	16	18
1968	16	18	16	20	9	20	14	13
1972	20	27	24	21	14	17	13	17
1976	18	23	19	22	12	19	13	22
1980	14	22	11	12	11	12	13	13
1984	15	22	15	10	9	16	14	13
1988	14	22	17	15	11	14	11	7
1992	13	21	15	13	6	11	11	14
1996	15	19	18	12	9	12	13	14
2000	22	33	24	18	17	19	20	19
2004	31	47	29	31	31	30	30	25
2008	33	49	39	34	19	31	25	24
2012	30	41	33	32	30	28	21	20
2016	23	36	27	23	19	19	16	17

(%) Contacted by Democratic Party

10 20 30 40

FIGURE 4.2 Voter Contact by the Democratic Party Overall and by Partisan Intensity (1956–2016) *Source*: Compiled by author from ANES Time Series Cumulative File (full samples, weighted).

Similar patterns show up again when the results are broken down by party. Figures 4.2 and 4.3 display contact rates by Democrats and Republicans respectively across the full 7-point partisan identification scale. Notably, pure independents and strong Democrats are both being contacted by Democrats at the same rate in 1956, and there are only incremental changes between the 1950s and the 1990s. In 1996, strong Democrats were contacted only slightly more than they had been forty years ago, at a rate of 19 percent on average, and independents are being contacted slightly less, at 9 percent. Once again, the real changes occur in 2000, with contact increasing across the board. For the Democrats, strong partisans (Democrats) are contacted at a rate that is 14 percentage points greater than in 1996, independents at a rate 8 percentage points greater, and even strong Republicans are contacted at a rate that is

Party Identification Intensity

Election Year	All Respondents	Strong Republican	Weak Republican	Leaning Republican	Independent	Leaning Democrat	Weak Democrat	Strong Democrat
1956	11	10	15	12	14	14	10	10
1960	14	24	17	18	16	9	9	10
1964	20	34	24	33	7	17	18	16
1968	18	23	20	26	15	17	15	16
1972	15	25	17	19	6	12	15	15
1976	15	30	20	20	10	13	10	14
1980	14	21	18	13	15	13	12	12
1984	13	17	15	15	9	9	8	15
1988	13	23	19	16	6	11	8	9
1992	11	16	15	13	6	11	8	9
1996	17	29	21	19	13	13	14	15
2000	25	38	26	30	14	18	24	25
2004	28	46	32	29	31	19	21	21
2008	25	40	33	32	12	20	21	19
2012	30	46	34	37	26	27	24	20
2016	18	34	20	21	16	12	12	14

(%) Contacted by Republican Party

10 20 30 40

FIGURE 4.3 Voter Contact by the Republican Party Overall and by Partisan Intensity (1956–2016) *Source:* Compiled by author from ANES Time Series Cumulative File (full samples, weighted).

5 percentage points higher on average, compared with the previous cycle. These findings imply Democrats amplified both their persuasion and base mobilization efforts over this period, but there is evidence that the focus on base partisans was more pronounced. I return to this later in the chapter.

For Republicans, the shift toward base mobilization over this period is also dramatic. Strong Republicans and pure independents are being contacted at almost the same rates in 1956, at 10 and 14 percent respectively. From 1996 to 2000, the contact rate for pure independents increases by only 1 percentage point. For leaning Republicans, the increase is substantial, rising by 11 percentage points, and contact among weak Republicans and strong Republicans also grows by 5 and 9 percentage points respectively, compared to pure independents. Similar patterns can be detected throughout the 2000s for Republicans. Strong Republicans are contacted at rates generally above 40 percent in three of the four most recent cycles (2004, 2008, and 2012), while contact rates for pure independents range from 12 to 30 percent on average in these elections. Like Democrats, Republicans over this period are also engaged in a fair amount of persuasion, boosting contact among strong, weak, and leaning Democrats between 1996 and 2000, in addition to base mobilization, but the initial evidence suggests the changes in Republican contacting strategies over this period reflect growing emphasis on reliable supporters rather than persuadable voters. In many ways, these findings are consistent with anecdotal accounts from the 2004 cycle, during which observers noted the Bush campaign did reach out to "discerning Democrats and wise independents," but as the campaign progressed, it spent more and more time on encouraging turnout and less and less on attempts to persuade the few undecided and cross-pressured voters (Goldstein 2004: A6; Stuckey 2005).

The pattern of comparatively greater focus on base mobilization becomes clearer when linear trends in contact rates by partisan identification, plotted visually in Figure 4.4, are examined. If political campaigns have shifted their attention increasingly to mobilizing base partisans, then we should observe rates of contact among strong partisans that disproportionately exceed contact rates for more persuadable voters, notably pure independents. The trends depicted in Figure 4.4 make precisely this case. The solid black (strong Republican) and solid gray (strong Democrat) lines exhibit the steepest slopes both in panel (a) (contact by either party) and respectively by party (panels b and c). Focusing on strong partisans and regressing the contact rates for this subgroup of voters on a time trend reveals contact by either party is climbing by 1.65 percentage points per cycle (standard error = .37, p = .001, two-tailed), on average, more than twice as fast as for pure independents, for whom contact is growing at a rate of .74 percentage points, on average (standard error = .39). Notably, the change among pure independents over time is just barely statistically significant, and only at the p = .08 level, using a two-tailed test.

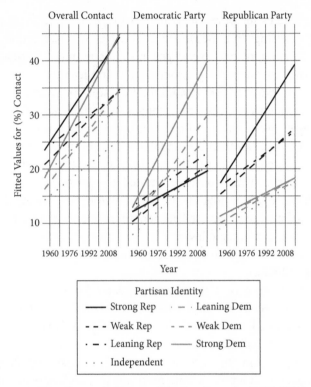

FIGURE 4.4 Voter Contact by Party and Partisan Intensity (1956–2016)
Source: Compiled by author from ANES Time Series Cumulative File (full samples, weighted).
Lines represent linear trends.

Earlier in the chapter, I argued that the 2000 election cycle represents a turning point with respect to campaign contacting strategies. This claim appears to be supported by the evidence I described, but I also consider the possibility of alternative cycles as turning points. I use time series analysis to investigate these possibilities by testing for structural breaks in the data. I perform tests of whether the coefficients in time series regressions vary over the periods defined by unknown break dates.[3] The procedure constructs a range of test statistics for structural breaks without imposing a known break date by combining the test statistics computed for each possible break date in the sample. For reported contact by either party among strong partisans overall, the analyses detect a structural break in the data in the 2000 cycle, as expected by the arguments developed earlier. The supremum Wald test statistic (14.4466, p = .0145) indicates we can reject the null hypothesis of no structural break and that the estimated break occurs in 2000.[4] Interestingly, parallel analyses suggest a structural break in reported Republican contact among strong Republicans also occurred in 2000,[5] while a break in reported Democratic contact among strong Democrats does not materialize until the 2004 cycle.[6] These results are consistent with the anecdotal accounts described earlier that Republicans were somewhat ahead of the curve on targeting base voters, starting in 2000, with Democrats following suit by the 2004 cycle. We explore these patterns further in the analyses that follow.

PARTISAN STRENGTH AND CAMPAIGN CONTACT: MULTIVARIATE ANALYSES

Next I examine these patterns more rigorously using multivariate approaches and consider more carefully the claims advanced about 2000 as a turning point in my study. My procedures are as follows. Since contact of any kind can be coded in its simplest form as a binary variable (contacted by Democrats and/or Republicans would be coded "1," while contacted by neither party would be a "0"), I can assign a one or a zero to each respondent in each election year. I then regress this binary variable on a measure of partisan intensity.

I expect that, in earlier years, partisanship will be less strongly correlated with contact, but in later years (especially after 2000), more intense partisans will be more likely to be contacted. I operationalize this expectation by creating an interaction term. The *year* variable is multiplied by the intensity of partisanship for each respondent, and this new variable is added to the model specification alongside the constituent variables. This approach allows me to detect whether the effect of partisanship increases or decreases linearly over time.

In Figure 4.5, I plot estimates of the predicted probabilities of contact by any major party since 1956 generated from a logistic regression model separately for strong partisans (the base) and pure independents (persuadable voters) to zoom in on this contrast (see Appendix Table A1 for details). The patterns are familiar. Contact for both categories of voters is on the mount over

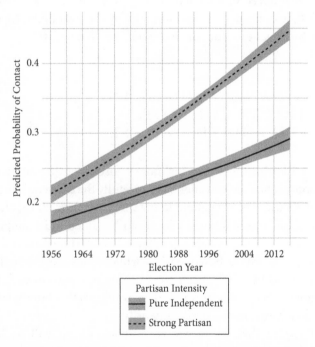

FIGURE 4.5 Predicted Probability of Voter Contact by Any Major Party for Strong Partisans and Pure Independents (1956–2016) *Source:* Compiled by author from ANES Time Series Cumulative File (full samples, weighted).

this period, but the rate at which strong partisans report contact outpaces the rate of reported contact by pure independents significantly. In 1956, the gap between the likelihood of contact reported by strong partisans and pure independents is relatively modest (about 4 percentage points); by 2016, the difference in the predicted probabilities of reported contact between strong partisans and pure independents is 16 percentage points, four times greater. A closer examination of the rates of change for each partisan subgroup reinforces this pattern. Between 1956 and 2016, the predicted likelihood of reported contact by either major party grows by 12 percentage points (from 17 to 29 percent) for pure independents, but, for strong partisans, the predicted likelihood increases at twice that rate—by 24 percentage points—from 21 to 45 percent over this period.

Next I incorporate my predicted change point at the 2000 election. I include a dichotomous variable equal to 0 in all elections before 2000, and 1 in 2000 and in all subsequent elections. By interacting this term with partisan intensity and adding these two new variables (both the dichotomous post-2000 indicator and its interaction with intensity) to the equations, I measure two new effects. First, I capture any shift in 2000 that was distinct from the overall linear trend; second, I examine any such shifts that affected respondents across varying levels of partisan intensity.

The visual evidence displayed in Figure 4.6 (Panel A) reveals a sharp leap in contact rates in 2000 (Brambor et al. 2006; see Appendix Table A2 for details).[7] This leap is so pronounced that it affects both independents and strong partisans, but the effect is more pronounced for strong partisans. The strong partisan contact predictions continue to climb even after 2000, but the independent line is shifting in the opposite direction, consistent with the hypothesis that base mobilization intensified starting in 2000, while the focus on persuadable voters dropped. Core partisan contact was climbing even before 2000, just as independent contact was shrinking before 2000, but the change in

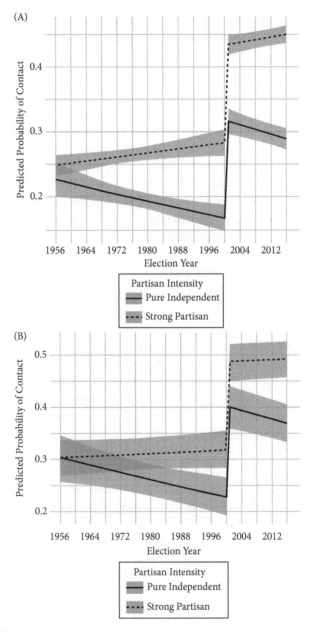

FIGURE 4.6 Predicted Probability of Voter Contact by Any Major Party Before and After 2000 for Strong Partisans and Pure Independents (1956–2016)

2000 affected each subgroup of voters differently. Controlling for a fuller range of demographic variables available in the cumulative ANES file (age, gender, race, education, religion, union membership, and marital status) to potentially improve the predictive power of the model and to reject alternative explanations suggests the model is robust to the inclusion of these additional controls and leaves the pattern essentially unchanged (Figure 4.6, Panel B; see Appendix Table A3 for details).

I leverage the fully specified estimation described earlier in the chapter to predict contact for each of the four partisan subgroups separately over this period. The results are displayed in Figure 4.7. For these analyses, I set all other variables to their

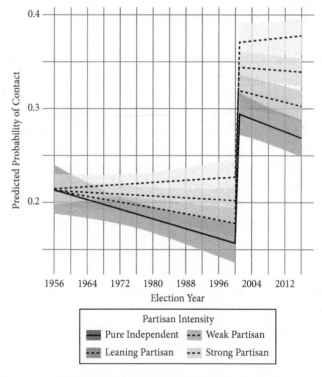

FIGURE 4.7 Predicted Probability of Voter Contact by Any Major Party by Partisan Intensity Before and After 2000 (1956–2016) *Source*: Compiled by author from ANES Time Series Cumulative File (full samples, weighted).

sample modes; accordingly, predicted probabilities are displayed for an average respondent, in this case, a white, married, Protestant, female, age 47, without union membership or an advanced degree.[8] Figure 4.7 reveals that predicted contact jumps overall for all categories of partisan intensity in 2000, but predicted contact since 2000 continues to rise only for strong partisans. The lines dip starting in 2000 and in subsequent cycles for weak and leaning partisans and—most dramatically and as expected—for pure independents.

PARTISAN DIFFERENCES IN CAMPAIGN CONTACT BEFORE AND AFTER 2000

Notwithstanding the patterns described in this chapter, there appear to be some differences across the two major parties in terms of their contacting strategies before and after 2000. In Figure 4.8, I display predicted probabilities of reported contact by either the Democratic or the Republican parties for strong partisan identifiers, respectively, and pure independents (see Appendix Table A4 for details). The plots show that both major parties have contacted their respective strong identifiers at higher rates over this period, relative to pure independents, and that strong identifiers in both parties report being contacted at significantly higher rates since 2000 overall compared with pure independents. In successive elections since 2000, however, contact overall continues to grow primarily for strong Democrats who reported being contacted by Democratic campaigns; by contrast, reported Republican contact by strong Republicans appears to have declined somewhat overall since 2000, as it has for pure independents.

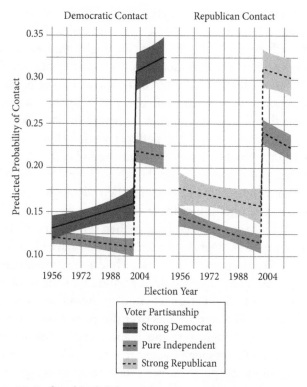

FIGURE 4.8 Predicted Probability of Voter Contact by Major Party and Partisan Intensity Before and After 2000 (1956–2016) *Source*: Compiled by author from ANES Time Series Cumulative File (full samples, weighted).

ZEROING IN ON THE BASE: TAKING IDEOLOGY INTO ACCOUNT

The analyses described in this chapter suggest presidential campaigns have been targeting their respective bases to a greater and greater extent over the past six decades and especially since 2000. These analyses have been based exclusively on grassroots

contact comparisons across levels of self-reported partisan identification. A finer-tuned delineation of the major parties' bases
can be achieved by taking voters' ideologies into account, in
addition to their partisan identities. Partisanship and ideology
are viewed as closely related but distinct concepts or belief systems. Scholars view political ideology as a "set of interrelated
attitudes that fit together in some coherent or consistent view
of or orientation toward the political world" (Flanigan et al.
2015: 168). A liberal orientation lies at one end of the ideological
spectrum, and conservative on the other. Since 1972, the ANES
has asked respondents to categorize their ideological positions
(as well as the intensity of these views), and most voters have
been able to do so consistently since then (Flanigan et al. 2015).
Consistently larger segments of the electorate have identified as
conservative, as opposed to liberal, while about one-quarter of
the population has regarded itself as middle-of-the-road ideologically since 1972 (Flanigan et al. 2015). About one-quarter to
one-third of ANES respondents over this period have reported
they "have not thought very much about this" (Flanigan et al.
2015). One could reasonably assert that respondents at the ends
of the ideological spectrum are more likely to comprise the
party bases. I exploit these classifications to zero in on the major
parties' respective bases and undertake a series of analyses to
examine whether respondents in these groups report higher
rates of contact since 1972.

Linear trends of reported contact by Democratic and
Republican campaigns for corresponding subgroups of voters
in presidential years are displayed in Figure 4.9. I compare reported Democratic contact for strong Democrats who also indicated they were "extremely liberal," strong Democrats who
identified as "moderate," and pure independents who were also
ideologically moderate. A parallel analysis is conducted for reported Republican contact across respective subgroups.

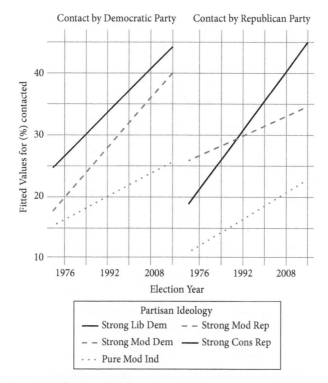

FIGURE 4.9 Predicted Probability of Voter Contact by Major Party, Partisan and Ideological Intensity (1972–2016) *Source*: Compiled by author from ANES Time Series Cumulative File (full samples, weighted). Lines represent linear trends.

The evidence reveals Democrats since 1972, and Republicans since the early 1990s, have consistently targeted strong partisans with extreme ideological views more so than moderate independents and even strong partisans who are moderate. Moreover, the reported rates of contact by both Democratic and Republican campaigns have grown more precipitously since 1972 for these highly targeted subgroups, relative to moderate independents and even strong partisans whose ideological views were moderate. These results strengthen the

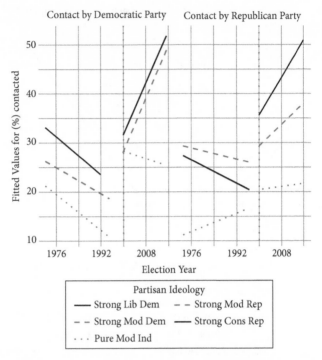

FIGURE 4.10 Predicted Probability of Voter Contact by Major Party, Partisan and Ideological Intensity Before and After 2000 (1972–2016) *Source*: Compiled by author from ANES Time Series Cumulative File (full samples, weighted). Lines represent linear trends.

claim that both major parties have focused increasingly on their respective bases over the past few decades.

Have these patterns changed since 2000? Figure 4.10 displays the trajectories of these patterns by corresponding voter subgroups before and since 2000. The evidence reveals the overall increases implied in Figure 4.9 reflect mainly the impact of developments since 2000. Before 2000, Democratic, but not Republican, campaigns focused more on strong partisans with extreme ideological outlooks, but the rates at which these voters report being contacted by each of the parties respectively were actually in decline on average for both parties. Strong, extreme partisans who identified with both political parties began to report increasingly higher rates of contact on average by both Democratic and Republican campaigns since 2000. Also since 2000, extremely conservative, strong Republicans have reported being contacted by Republican campaigns at higher rates on average compared with moderate independents and moderate, strong Republicans. By contrast, moderate independents report being contacted at lower rates by Democrats, as expected, and at only slightly higher rates on average by Republicans, since 2000.

These additional analyses refining the conceptualization of the party bases to incorporate ideological orientations in addition to partisan identification reinforce the basic findings reported throughout this chapter, specifically, that both major parties have increasingly targeted their respective bases in recent decades, and that this pattern has accelerated since 2000.

CONCLUSION

One observer has noted that "no campaign can hope to succeed without first activating its core supporters" (Stuckey 2005: 154). By and large, presidential campaigns appear to have internalized this dictum, but the extent to which they have been reaching beyond the base in recent years is debatable. The analyses presented in this chapter underscore two basic findings. First, the assessments of voter contact strategies reported by respondents in the ANES reveal strong partisans have been targeted at increasingly higher rates since 2000, relative to pure independent voters. This appears to be true for contact by either party overall and contact only by the Democratic or Republican parties. I interpret these results to be more consistent with base maximization, rather than base expansion, strategies, as I have defined these in this chapter. Second, the findings suggest empirical support for the contention that the 2000 election represents a turning point that appears to have accelerated a heightened focus on the party bases in presidential elections. In subsequent chapters, I will consider the implications of these shifts for policymaking and democracy in America. The following chapter, however, presents some additional material that reinforces the shift in the focus of campaign targets described in this chapter.

PRIMING THE PARTY

Labels are devices for saving talkative persons the trouble
of thinking.

—JOHN MORLEY

Labels cloud our vision and distract us from seeing
how much we have in common with one another.

—RUSSELL SIMMONS

HUMAN BEINGS ARE COGNITIVE MISERS, striving to expend
as little cognitive effort as possible on routine tasks. Because
individuals are limited in our capacity to process information,
we take shortcuts wherever we can (Fiske and Taylor 1984).
Party labels function as shortcuts, or heuristics, enabling voters
to simplify the way they think about the complex political world
and to make sound choices without the costly acquisition of detailed or encyclopedic information (Popkin 1991; Lupia 1994).
But partisan labels also divide politics and voters into in-groups
(us) and out-groups (them) and foster the formation of social
identities around them that promote in-group loyalty *über alles*
(Green, Palmquist, and Schickler 2004). These labels can be
used to great effect to galvanize support among co-partisans by
invoking shared social identity (Foos and de Rooji 2017; Walsh
2004), even as they risk alienating other voters. As such, the del-
icate ways in which party labels are used in campaign appeals
can reveal a great deal about strategic priorities.

In the previous chapter, I exploited self-reported survey
data on voter contact over time to investigate changing patterns

Bases Loaded. Costas Panagopoulos, Oxford University Press (2021). © Oxford University Press.
DOI: 10.1093/oso/9780197533062.001.0001.

in presidential campaign strategies over the past six decades. Taken as a whole, the evidence suggests that campaigns have targeted base partisans at increasingly higher rates compared with pure independents and partisans of less intense identification in recent years (and especially since the 2000 election cycle). As I discussed in Chapter 4, reports of voter contact represent indirect measures of campaign strategy; direct, reliable, and consistent measures over time are not readily available. In this chapter, I turn to an alternative source of evidence—contents of television advertisements in presidential campaigns—to glean any additional insights about shifts in campaign strategy over the past sixty years or so. These data are also imperfect, as I discuss further later in the chapter, but they do offer some advantages, including the fact that they could be viewed as more direct indicators of campaign strategies since decisions about ads content are made by the campaigns themselves, including campaigns waged independently by parties and special interest groups operating in presidential races. The limitations associated with the evidence I describe lead me to caution readers to adopt a circumspect interpretation; I consider the findings to be mainly speculative or suggestive. Overall, however, the patterns I detect in the analyses that follow largely point in a similar direction: presidential campaigns are increasingly targeting their respective bases in campaigns, as demonstrated by the growing rate at which overt partisan cues are imbedded in their direct appeals to voters broadcasted on cable and network television.

TELEVISION ADVERTISING IN CAMPAIGNS

Campaigns spend most of their money on political advertising (Panagopoulos 2017). Presidential campaigns in recent cycles have devoted large chunks of their overall spending budget on television advertising in particular. Studies of television advertisements have found that the number of the general election (September–Election Day) airings in presidential campaigns has been on the rise, doubling, for example, between the 2008 and 2012 cycle (from 310,000 airings in the top-100 media markets to 635,000 respectively) (Motta and Fowler 2016). Moreover, the 2020 political cycle is projected to hit an all-time record—as high as $10 billion—in spending on political ads (Montellaro 2019; Wilson 2019). By February 2020, political ad spending had already reached about $7 billion, representing a 63 percent increase compared with the 2015–2016 season in total (eMarketer 2020). Most of the ads broadcast on television are negative in tone, especially in presidential races and those sponsored by parties and interest groups (Ridout and Franz 2011). Nearly three-in-four television ads aired during the general election in 2008 were negative, for instance, and this figure grew to 87 percent of airings in the race between Democratic President Obama and Republican nominee Mitt Romney in 2012 (Motta and Fowler 2016).

Despite the massive spending on political messaging via television ads, the political science literature has not reached a consensus regarding the effectiveness of these missives. In this chapter, I present an overview of what scholars have had to say about the impact and the nature of political advertising. I then discuss some pertinent developments in the contents of television ads in presidential elections as they relate to the arguments advanced in this book. Specifically, I examine whether elements of presidential campaign ads on television reflect the shift in strategic focus toward base partisans, compared with independents or persuadable voters, in recent election cycles that I have documented earlier in this chapter for other areas.

As I noted, early studies regarding the impact of the campaign messaging were done by Lazarsfeld, Berelson, and Gaudet (1944). The so-called Columbia studies intended to examine the consumer-like behavior of the electorate, where voters evaluate different candidates and choose the one that seems most beneficial to them. From this perspective, political advertising should play an important role in informing voters about candidates' positions on various policies. Contrary to their expectations in the 1940 presidential election, however, the authors discovered a strong level of brand loyalty among the electorate based on their belongingness to specific social groups, including parties (Lazarsfeld et al., 1944). They found that people rarely changed their minds regarding presidential choice. The authors concluded campaign messages, like media more generally, exert only "minimal effects" and are more likely to reinforce initial voters' preferences rather than change minds. Nevertheless, it is important to mention that Lazarsfeld and his colleagues did find some persuasive impact of political ads on a small portion of independent voters. Similarly, Hovland (1959) found that only a few people actually update their attitudes because of their exposure to political ads.

Further research reinforced the "minimal effects" thesis of media messages on voters' opinions. One explanation for these findings was based on the fact that voters tend to expose themselves selectively to the messages they already agree with in the first place (Klapper 1960). Another explanation was posited by authors of the "Michigan model" who showed that most of the voters possess little knowledge about political matters and pay little attention to political information (Campbell et al. 1960). Therefore, in their decisions about preferred political candidates, voters rely more on their party attachments rather than on any information to which they were exposed during the campaign.

Over time, scholars challenged the "minimal effects" thesis by arguing, in part, that, although political ads may not change voters' minds easily, they can shape what voters care about during the election cycle (Krosnick and Kinder 1990).

In other words, political messaging can shape the salience of the issues voters use to choose among candidates in an election. Furthermore, Bartels (1993) showed that exposure to political messaging can alter issue positions.

Other scholars demonstrated that even though political ads generally have limited impact on the general public, they do affect specific subgroups of voters more strongly. For instance, Zaller (1992) found that media messages can have an impact on voters with moderate levels of political sophistication. He argued that such voters pay adequate attention to political information but have fewer party predispositions. This combination of political interest and weak alignment with any of the major parties makes these voters more susceptible to political messaging. In more recent studies, scholars found that voters with lower levels of political knowledge are the most susceptible to political messaging (Franz and Ridout 2007).

One of the problems in uncovering the impact of political ads is the possibility that due to the competitive nature of political campaigns, the impact of political ads from each side cancels each other out (Zaller 1996). In other words, if voters were exposed to approximately the same volume of political messages from each side, the overall effect of all these messages will be close to zero. This logic may explain why, for a long time, scholars were struggling to find any observable impact of political ads. Another potential obstacle of campaign ad impact is the difficulty in controlling the level of exposure to political messaging. Scholars struggle to develop reliable measures of different levels of individual exposure to political ads. For instance, Shaw (1999) examined the impact of political ads in presidential campaigns in 1988, 1992, and 1996 and found that increases in political advertising on the state level led to an increase in the vote-share for the candidates that placed the ads. One limitation of such studies, however, lies in the inability to control the variation in exposure within the state (some countries received more advertising while others less). Additionally, researchers have to account for all sources of political ads, whether they come from candidates themselves or from other actors that support or oppose their candidacies. Shaw addressed most of these issues in a later study (2006) and found a much weaker impact of political ads in the 2000 and 2004 presidential campaigns. Eventually, a groundbreaking randomized experiment conducted in collaboration with an actual gubernatorial campaign in Texas showed that television ads had the capacity to persuade voters, but the effects were modest and short-lived, dissipating within a matter of a few days at best (Gerber et al. 2011).

These studies made tremendous advances in how we think about political advertising in campaigns. One refinement focused on the conceptualization of ad impact. Ridout and Franz (2011), for instance, suggested a conceptual distinction between two different forms of persuasion: direct and indirect. Direct persuasion refers to an update in vote choice in response to political ad exposure, while indirect persuasion refers to an impact on the likelihood to turn out on Election Day. An ad can have a positive or negative indirect effect. For example, specific political messaging can mobilize support for a candidate and bring voters to the polls or suppress support for an opponent. By airing negative information about an opponent, political actors can decrease the willingness of the opponent's supporters to turn out.

The effect of negative ads has been at the center of scholarly debates for decades, in part since the lion's share of all political ads in U.S. presidential elections are negative. Does this mean that political ads are the reason for relatively low turnout in the United States compared with other developed democracies? Indeed scholars have found evidence in the laboratory that negative ads can be linked to decreased turnout (Ansolabehere and Iyengar 1995), but more recent studies have rejected these findings and argued that the negative political ads have no depressing impact on turnout (Franz and Ridout 2007; Krasno and Green 2008). In an attempt to explain conflicting evidence from different studies Krupnikov (2011, 2014) shows that negative ads can indeed depress turnout but only if voters were exposed to these ads after making up their minds. Other studies find that negative ads actually focus on salient political issues (Geer 2006) more than positive ads, are more memorable (Mattes and Redlawsk 2014), and significantly boost voter knowledge about candidate positions (Morey 2017; Freedman, Franz, and Goldstein 2004). Indeed, Mattes and Redlawsk (2014) have argued that negative advertising is not necessarily detrimental and may be needed to convey valuable information that would not otherwise be revealed.

In recent years, as I have discussed throughout, advances in ad targeting capabilities have transformed the communication landscape in elections. Before these developments, all voters more or less were exposed to similar political content (Prior 2007; Hamilton 2005). Before the 1980s, the three television networks (ABC, NBC, and CBS) presented information in a similar manner due to the fairness doctrine of the FCC that required honest, equitable, and balanced representation of all political information. During this period, political ads were created to appeal to all voters (the so-called shotgun approach). However, with the cancelation of the fairness doctrine in 1987, and the development of cable, satellite, and Internet technologies, there has been gradual audience segmentation by political views (e.g., Fox News), information interests (e.g., CNN or ESPN), and geographical location (since satellite technology allows smaller stations to cover major stories) (Hamilton, 2005). These developments also allow political actors and media consultants to develop strategies of tailor-made political messaging for the target audiences (Motta and Flower 2016; Hersh and Schaffner 2013; Ridout et al. 2012). Indeed, since the onset of television audience segmentation, political campaigners have been able to identify distinct viewers of specific programs and target political ads by age or gender (Mann 2011), political affiliation (Ridout et al. 2012), or general interests (Lovett and Peress 2010). Further development of social networks and online media allows even more nuanced targeting of the voters. In recent years, we can see a gradual shift from the use of television advertising toward digital media (Franz et al. 2020), where campaigns can use even more sophisticated targeting. Most recently, the advent of addressable television, which enables campaigns to target ads to individual households rather than geographic media markets, also facilitates greater precision in targeting capacity that increasingly resembles what was previously available only by media options, like direct mail, that allowed narrowcasting of messages (Motta and Folwer 2016).

Some scholars have linked developments in the media and television landscape to political polarization. In the past having a limited number of channels that were regulated by the government to present a more measured picture of political reality served as a "great equalizer" in terms of political knowledge (Prior 2007). Even people who were not interested in politics had no choice but to consume some amounts of political information that presumably made them more knowledgeable and better equipped to make more informed political choices. Viewers can now bypass such content at the click of a button. At the same time, other viewers can chose to consume massive amounts of political content. Since the content itself has become less regulated in terms of balanced views, outlets have diverged from each other in how they interpret and present political news. Conservative and Republican audiences now prefer to receive their news from Fox News, while liberals and Democrats turn instead to NPR, CNN, and MSNBC (Iyengar and Hahn 2009). As a result, in the United States, audiences are not interested in or knowledgeable about politics, or they are very attentive to political information that comes from more and more polarized sources. Greater partisan polarization makes it harder for campaign strategists to use ads that aim to persuade voters to support specific candidates.

In such a scenario, it is reasonable to expect that campaigns would prefer not to waste resources to attempt to persuade highly polarized viewers but would rather shift their efforts to mobilization. Does the content of political advertising in presidential campaigns support the contention developed throughout this book that presidential campaigns have shifted their attention away from persuadable voters and toward base partisans in recent elections? One manifestation of such a shift would be that presidential television ads increasingly feature more partisan cues, such as explicit mentions of political party labels or affiliations. Voters routinely rely on partisan cues as information shortcuts in political campaigns (Panagopoulos 2017; Popkin 1991), but including party labels in broadcasted appeals can also backfire by alienating independent voters or even rival partisans. Campaigns would be less concerned about such backlash, however, if their focus were on the base. Recent experimental studies have shown that partisan cues effectively mobilize party supporters (the base) compared with rival partisans (Foos and de Rooji 2017).

TELEVISION AD CONTENT AND CAMPAIGN STRATEGY

Researchers have culled ad content for decades to decipher campaign strategies. These studies have yielded important insights. For example, the studies have shown that television ads in presidential elections are predominantly negative in tone (Motta and Fowler 2016) and sometimes focus more on personal qualities than on substantive policy issues (West 2018). In the 2008 election, for example, John McCain, the Republican nominee, devoted extensive attention to attacking Obama's inexperience (West 2018: 43). In fact, West (2018) found that nearly half of all prominent presidential ads in the 2008 cycle focused on personal dimensions rather than policy.

Despite these, and related pioneering studies (Geer 2006), rigorous analyses of presidential ad content over time can be methodologically challenging because systematic and comprehensive coding of ad content is unavailable. To investigate trends in party mentions in presidential television ads over the course of the current study, I leverage several sources of available data. One source of information about the contents of presidential advertisements broadcasted on television is the data collected and compiled by the Wesleyan Media Project (WMP) (2012 and 2016), formerly the Wisconsin Advertising Project (WAP) (2000–2008).[1] Beginning in 1998, these projects used technology developed by the Campaign Media Analysis Group (CMAG) to track political advertisements that aired on broadcast and cable television stations across the United States. For 2000, the data covers the nation's seventy-five largest media markets; by 2004, the top-100 media markets were included. And since 2008, all 210 media markets in the United States are included. These databases represent the most detailed and comprehensive source of information about political ads broadcasted on television available. Researchers have access to storyboards of each individual ad aired (along with details about when ads aired, on which stations or shows, etc.), which enabled them to identify a wide range of ad features, including ad sponsor, tone, policy content, and other elements. Crucially, WAP/WMP researchers coded whether ads aired in presidential elections mentioned the candidates' party affiliations.

Analyses of the WAP/WMP data reveal general election television ads aired in presidential elections rarely include partisan cues. On average, starting in the 2000 cycle, nearly 94 percent of all television ads that aired in the corresponding media markets during the general election (September 1–Election Day) did not include any mention of party affiliations. This is consistent with findings reported in Motta and Fowler (2016), as well as in earlier, similar studies that found that only 1 percent of prominent television ads in presidential races between 1952–2008 included party mentions (West 2013).

A closer look at party content in recent cycles, however, tells an intriguing story. Figure 5.1 plots the share of presidential advertisements aired during general elections between 2000 and 2016 that included party mentions. In 2000, about 3.5 percent of these ads mentioned parties. By 2016, that figure more than doubled, to about 7.4 percent of ads aired. Although there are only a limited number of data points (and none prior to 2000 are available), the evidence shows a modest uptick overall

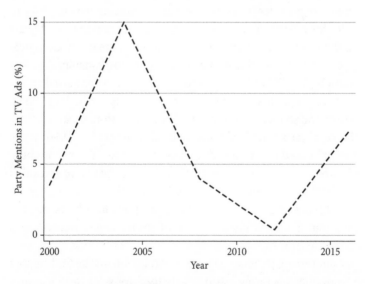

FIGURE 5.1 Party Mentions in Presidential Ads Aired on Television (2000–2016) *Source:* Wisconsin Advertising Project (WAP) (2000–2008); Wesleyan Media Project (WMP) (2012, 2016). General election ads only (September 1–Election Day).

in the share of ads that mentioned candidates' party affiliations in four out of the five presidential cycles that followed 2000. In 2004, the spike (to about 15 percent of ads aired) was quite pronounced, but the frequency of party mentions recoiled to 4 percent in 2008 and then dropped to 0.5 percent in 2012 (when clearly very few such mentions were included) before jumping to 7.4 percent in 2016. I hesitate to extract too much from this analysis, but the overall pattern is consistent with the other evidence presented in this book that suggests campaigns are increasingly shifting their emphasis toward partisans and away from persuadable (or independent) voters in recent election cycles, even in television advertisements that are exposed to broad audiences.

For a longer term perspective on these patterns, I supplement the WAP/WMP data (for cycles 2000–2016) with parallel information obtained from Darrell West's (2013) analyses of the content of presidential television ads for cycles between 1956 and 1996, for a total of sixteen presidential election cycles.[2] Figure 5.2 depicts the complete series. Admittedly, the methodological approaches across the studies differ, perhaps considerably. For example, WAP/WMP data reflect the share of ads aired in respective media markets with party mentions, while West's data denote the share of prominent ads that mentioned party labels. The original sources of these data also differ. For 1956–1988, they are based on Jamieson's (1996) descriptions of presidential ads aired on television. For 1992–1996, the data were compiled by West based on TV ads that aired during the news coverage on the *CBS Evening News*. Neither is a complete list of ads, just the ones that achieved some degree of prominence. Accordingly, I urge caution in interpreting the results, but, once more, several interesting patterns emerge. First, I confirm the finding that presidential ads rarely feature party mentions. Since 1956, party mentions appear in fewer than 4 percent of presidential television ads on average. Over the duration of this period, however,

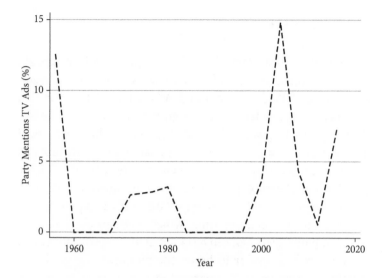

FIGURE 5.2 Party Mentions in Presidential Ads Aired on Television (1956–2016) *Sources:* Jamieson (1996) (1956–1988); West (2013) (1992, 1996); Wisconsin Advertising Project (WAP) (2000–2008); Wesleyan Media Project (WMP) (2012, 2016); WAP/WMP: general election ads only (September 1–Election Day).

analysis of the series reveals the frequency of party mentions has likely grown modestly (by about .13 percentage points on average per cycle). Although I note this pattern is not statistically significant at conventional levels, it supports the notion that presidential campaigns are increasingly featuring party cues in ads aired on television. Consistent with a central argument advanced throughout this book, there is also evidence of a more pronounced—and statistically significant—shift since 2000 (regressing the series on a time trend and an indicator for the five most recent cycles yields a coefficient of 8.2 (standard error = 3.7) for the indicator (p = .04, two-tailed). In fact, the share of ads that mentioned parties was nearly five times greater on average in election cycles starting in 2000 (about 6.1 percent) compared with prior years (about 1.3 percent).

CONCLUSION

Analyses of partisan rhetoric on the U.S. presidential campaign trail over time have yielded mixed results about the inclusion of party cues. While Rhodes and Albert (2017) find partisan statements in presidential campaign rhetoric to be on the decline in general between 1952 and 2012, mainly due to a marked decrease in the rate Democratic partisan appeals (Republican candidates rarely invoked party labels over this period), Tiplady (2019) shows the use of party mentions in presidential campaign rhetoric to be on the rise between 1960 and 2012. In presidential campaign television advertising, which, perhaps even more so than campaign speeches, can be targeted to receptive audiences, partisan appeals appear to be on the mount, however. Taken together, the evidence summarized in this chapter implies the shift toward base partisans, relative to moderate or independent voters documented throughout this book in other presidential campaign domains manifests, at least to some extent, in the contents of television ads aired in these races. Growing reliance on party cues in these ads is presumably designed to activate partisan sentiment and predispositions and to mobilize voters on the basis of these allegiances. By contrast, such party cues are likely irrelevant for independents or unaffiliated voters who lack partisan affinities.

Framing political messages in partisan terms can have important implications for how citizens interpret, understand, and react to the political world (Walsh 2004). It is widely recognized that people interpret politics through the frames used by elites (Walsh 2004). If elites are framing political messages increasingly in ways that emphasize their partisan elements, these frames can cause individuals to develop or reinforce collective, partisan, social identities that influence their outlooks on political issues and even constrain the considerations they use to communicate about politics (Walsh 2004: 170). As Walsh (2004: 171) argues, "identities interact with interests and principles to influence individuals' interpretations of politics." Priming partisan considerations in campaigns appeals will only calcify citizens' partisan social identities, cause them to view the political world in increasingly partisan terms, and intensify identity-based politics.

TURNING OUT OR

TUNING OUT?

We do not have government by the majority.
We have government by the majority who participate.

—THOMAS JEFFERSON

WHO WINS ELECTIONS IS DETERMINED by who votes. Who votes is often dictated by campaigns and the strategies they devise to pursue victory. Turnout matters in elections, and there is an inextricable link between campaign strategy and which voters show up at the polls on Election Day. The empirical analyses presented so far in the preceding chapters of this book suggest base partisans are being targeted at increasingly higher rates in recent presidential campaigns, relative to persuadable, swing, or independent voters. The ramifications of these changes extend broadly, affecting political participation and, ultimately, public policy and the nature of representative democracy in America. In this chapter, I focus on the consequences of shifting campaign targets on electoral participation.

CHANGING CAMPAIGN TARGETING STRATEGIES AND VOTER TURNOUT

Despite the fact that democracy depends on citizens exercising their right to vote, people are often surprised that so many

Bases Loaded. Costas Panagopoulos, Oxford University Press (2021). © Oxford University Press.
DOI: 10.1093/oso/9780197533062.001.0001.

Americans often fail to vote in elections. Even in high-profile, high-salience presidential election years, large swaths of eligible voters fail to vote. Figure 6.1 depicts turnout rates among eligible voters in presidential general elections over the period of this study (1956 to 2016).[1] Turnout has waxed and waned over time, averaging 58 percent of eligible voters nationally; at no point did more than 64 percent participate in these election cycles. This means more than two-in-five eligible voters on average fail to register their preferences on Election Day. Consider that, in the 2012 presidential election in which there were 221,925,820 eligible voters in the United States, the overall turnout rate was 58.2 percent, implying that 92,854,914 potential voters provided no input into the selection of the president of the United States. In some years, that figure is even higher (Panagopoulos and Weinschenk 2015).

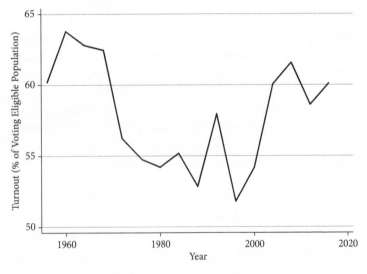

FIGURE 6.1 Turnout Among Eligible Voters (1956–2016) *Source:* McDonald (2016).

Given the centrality of voting in a democracy, it is unsurprising that scholars have devoted considerable attention to explaining why some people vote while others do not. Rational choice theorists have argued that, when deciding whether to vote, potential voters calculate the expected utility of voting (what they gain voting) and whether the benefits exceed costs (Aldrich 1995; Downs 1957; Olson 1965). This approach is rooted in economics, a field that assumes people make decisions about consumer purchases by weighing the benefits against the costs. By this logic, voting may be irrational because the costs associated with it, however small, will almost certainly outweigh any policy benefits once the latter are discounted by the likelihood of being the pivotal voter in any given election (basically zero). To reconcile this expectation with the fact that at least some voters participate in almost every election, Riker and Ordeshook (1968) argued that voters take factors beyond costs and benefits into account, and may engage in voting, even if costs outweigh the benefits, to express themselves or to perform their civic duty. This perspective asserts that voting is likely shaped by perceptions of appropriate behavior (such as social norms and conforming to the expectations of others); personal psychological factors (e.g., sense of civic duty); or solidary, purposive, or selective benefits (such as the satisfaction derived from working with like-minded people or toward a policy goal, respectively, even if the goal is not achieved). These motivations are sufficient to overcome cost-benefit calculations even if an individual's vote is not pivotal (Panagopoulos and Weinschenk 2015).

An alternative set of explanations focus on the role of resources. Brady, Verba, and Schlozman (1995), for example, argue that decisions to engage around three sets of resources— time (to participate), money (to donate to political candidates, parties, and causes), and civic skills. Civic skills refer to communication and organizational abilities (e.g., the ability to speak in public, to write well, to lead groups, etc.) Brady et al. (1995) demonstrate that these resources play an important role in shaping individuals' political participation decisions and that those who are socioeconomically advantaged are more likely to have the time, money, and civic skills to vote (Panagopoulos and Weinschenk 2015).

A wide range of additional perspectives on voting behavior is advanced in this literature, including many studies that focus on the role of structural features, electoral rules, and other institutions in shaping turnout (Cox 1999), as well as sociopsychological incentives to vote, like complying with social voting norms and performing ones' civic duty (Blais 2000). One finding is especially noteworthy and relevant to the current project. Rosenstone and Hansen (1993) have emphasized the role of mobilization, showing that voters are significantly more likely to vote when they are asked to do so. In fact, the authors explain that the decline in voter turnout between the 1960s and the 1990s was attributable mainly to declining voter mobilization efforts (especially by parties and groups like unions) during this period (Rosenstone and Hansen 1993). There is considerable evidence that voter mobilization tends to raise political engagement and participation levels, and some evidence suggests the impact of grassroots mobilization is growing stronger in recent election cycles (Panagopoulos and Francia 2009).

If voter contact is linked so closely with voting decisions, any inequalities or disparities in mobilization can have important consequences. In previous chapters, I argued and demonstrated that political campaigns have enhanced their targeting of base partisans in recent election cycles. If Rosenstone and Hansen (1993) are correct, this shift in mobilization targets has likely boosted participation among strong partisans disproportionately compared with other partisan subgroups, and especially persuadable voters.

To undertake this analysis empirically, I turn once again to the ANES, which has collected self-reported data on voting in presidential elections between 1956 and 2016. I recognize social desirability generally causes respondents to inflate their voting reports in surveys (Panagopoulos 2017), but I expect any such effects will not vary much across the time period in my study. Figure 6.2 displays turnout rates for cycles over this period for respondents overall and by subgroups of partisan intensity.

The estimates presented in Figure 6.2 confirm that observed turnout rises with partisan intensity. Approximately 55 percent of pure independents report voting in these election cycles on average. Leaning and weak partisans report voting at higher and roughly comparable rates—73 and 74 percent respectively on average over this period. By contrast, 86 percent of strong partisans report voting on average in these election years.

			Partisan Intensity		
		All Respondents	Independents	Leaning Partisans	Weak Partisans	Strong Partisans
	1956	76	77	74	72	80
	1960	81	74	79	80	85
	1964	79	62	76	77	84
	1968	77	65	76	75	84
	1972	73	50	74	74	83
	1976	72	55	73	70	85
Election Year	1980	71	49	72	70	85
	1984	74	55	70	73	86
	1988	70	45	64	68	84
	1992	75	56	73	75	86
	1996	73	42	67	70	89
	2000	73	48	69	72	86
	2004	77	49	71	78	89
	2008	78	48	71	81	92
	2012	78	53	77	76	90
	2016	76	49	76	75	88

(%) Voter Turnout   50 60 70 80 90

FIGURE 6.2 Self-Reported Voter Turnout for All Respondents and by Partisan Intensity (1956–2016) *Source*: Compiled by author from ANES Time Series Cumulative File (full samples, weighted).

Closer inspection of the trends implied by these data reveals some intriguing patterns. Linear trends of the observed turnout rates by partisan intensity are displayed in Figure 6.3. Regressing turnout rates on a time counter shows there was no meaningful change overall (all respondents) (coefficient = −.05 (standard error = .17), p = .78, two-tailed) for this time period, but things look quite different upon replicating this analysis for respective categories of partisan intensity. The results reveal no significant changes for leaning (coefficient = −.24, standard error = .21, p = .27, two-tailed) or weak partisans (coefficient = .09, standard error = .21, p = .68, two-tailed). By contrast, the rate at which pure independent voters have reported voting has *declined* significantly over this period (by about 1.6 percentage points on average each cycle) (coefficient = −1.55, standard error = .38,

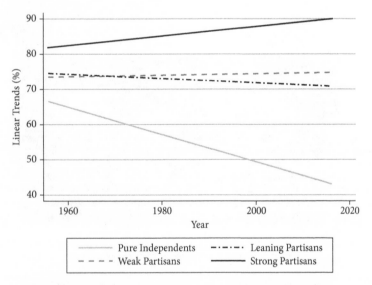

FIGURE 6.3 Reported Voter Turnout Trends by Partisan Intensity (1956–2016) *Source:* Compiled by author from ANES Time Series Cumulative File (full samples, weighted). Lines represent linear trends.

$p = .001$, two-tailed), while self-reported turnout among strong partisans has *grown* significantly on average over time (by about .53 percentage points per cycle) (coefficient = .53, standard error = .09, $p = .00$, two-tailed). Zooming in on the difference between the observed (self-reported) turnout rates reported by strong partisans and pure independents, the linear trend displayed in Figure 6.4 confirms the robust, upward trajectory over the past six decades.

How much of the growth in turnout among strong partisans over this period can be attributed to increased contact by political campaigns? Disentangling the causal relationship between voter contact and turnout using observational data is methodologically challenging because likely voters tend to be targeted by campaigns (Francia and Panagopoulos 2009). Microtargeting clearly enables campaigns to decipher voting propensities in

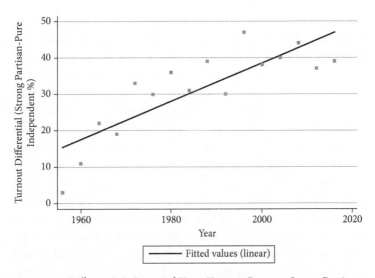

FIGURE 6.4 Differences in Reported Voter Turnout Between Strong Partisans and Pure Independents (1956–2016) *Source*: Compiled by author from ANES Time Series Cumulative File (full samples, weighted). Line represents linear trend.

advance, and campaigns take these into account when devising targeting strategies (Francia and Panagopoulos 2009; Beck and Heidemann 2014). It is unclear, therefore, whether turnout among strong partisans is growing because these voters are being mobilized at higher rates or whether these voters are being mobilized more precisely because they were more likely to vote in the first place. But it is also likely that the mobilization efforts lavished on these voters reinforces or cements their likelihood to do so, exerting strong, independent effects on whether these voters ultimately participate, as hundreds of randomized field experiments have shown (Panagopoulos 2011; Green and Gerber 2012). While these tensions are not fully resolved, my main goal is to illustrate there are clear differences in voter participation trends across categories of partisan intensity between 1956 and 2016. I argue these differences are linked, at least in part, to changing strategies of voter contacting and targeting over this period.

To examine this possibility empirically, if only crudely, I display the simple, bivariate correlations between reported contact and reported voter turnout separately for strong partisans and pure independents in Figure 6.5. The relationships are clearly very different. The analyses reveal a strong and highly statistically-significant correspondence between contact and turnout for strong partisans (Pearson's R = .79, p = .0002), but virtually no relationship for pure independents. In fact, the bivariate correlation for pure independents is actually negative (Pearson's R = −.13, p = .63) and statistically insignificant, implying turnout is unrelated to contact among pure independents. It seems whether independents vote on Election Day has little to do with whether they were contacted during the campaign and more to do with other factors. As I noted, I concede correlation does not imply causation, but the patterns are nevertheless intriguing (and confirmed by more rigorous, multivariate

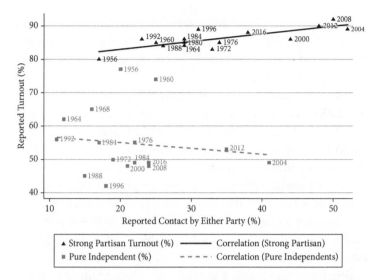

FIGURE 6.5 Comparing the Turnout-Contact Relationship Between Strong Partisans and Pure Independents (1956–2000) *Source*: Compiled by author from ANES Time Series Cumulative File (full samples, weighted). Lines represent linear trends.

analyses; details upon request) and consistent with the notion that the growth in targeting has likely boosted turnout rates among strong partisans, while voting by pure independents is unrelated to contact. The results are also consistent with re-analyses of experimental data that show that mobilization interventions exert larger effects among voters with high-voting propensities, compared to low-propensity voters, like pure independents who are expected to vote at relatively lower rates (Enos, Fowler, and Vavreck 2014).

Given these findings, it is perhaps unsurprising that presidential campaigns may have decided it is inefficient—perhaps even counterproductive—to focus on mobilizing persuadable voters in elections. The evidence suggests campaigns' efforts among independent voters likely fall on deaf ears. The solution, however, is not necessarily to overlook these voters, as campaigns seem to be doing more and more, but rather to find impactful and effective ways to reach out to them. Campaigns need to find new approaches to break through to these voters, not simply write them off.

Another claim advanced throughout this book is that the 2000 election reshaped the nature of targeting by political campaigns and has exerted enduring effects on campaign strategy in presidential elections. To what extent does this impact manifest in observed voting in elections? I estimate a logistic regression model to predict self-reported voting as a function of change over time and incorporated an indicator to capture the effects of the 2000 election and cycles that follow (see Appendix Table A5 for details). The estimates were used to calculate predicted probabilities of voting for voters across the range of partisan intensity separately, which are plotted in Figure 6.6. The evidence suggests a bump in reported turnout across the board since 2000, but turnout only climbs reliably for strong partisans since the 2000 election. Self-reported turnout after 2000 for other partisan subgroups either remains unchanged (weak partisans) or declines (weak partisans and pure independents). This additional evidence implies the 2000 election cycle was also a turning point for turnout in presidential elections, with enduring consequences, buoying participation by the base almost exclusively.

The shifting patterns of reported participation by categories of partisan intensity described has had significant, and potentially long-lasting, implications for democracy in America. One consequence has been that these changes appear to have reshaped the constellation of the composition of the voting electorate. Figure 6.7 shows that strong partisans increasingly represent a larger and larger share of the electorate (about 40 percent of those who report voting in the most recent cycles, compared

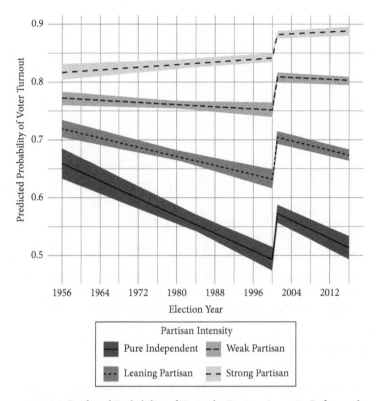

FIGURE 6.6 Predicted Probability of Voting by Partisan Intensity Before and After 2000 (1956–2016) *Source*: Compiled by author from ANES Time Series Cumulative File (full samples, weighted).

with less than 30 percent in the late 1970s and early 1980s), while the share of voters who identify as pure independents has declined. The Lowess-smoothed curve depicted in Figure 6.7 represents the pattern of the difference between the share of strong partisans and pure independents between 1956 and 2016 and implies the balance has favored strong partisans, and that this advantage, in terms of comprising a larger share of voters, has grown consistently since the 1980s.

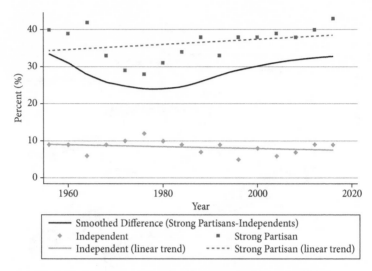

FIGURE 6.7 Composition of Electorate by Strength of Partisan Identification (1956–2016) *Source*: Compiled by author using ANES Cumulative File (full samples, weighted). Among those who reported voted only. Lines represent linear trends.

CONCLUSION

This chapter examined voter turnout patterns over time in presidential elections and showed there are significant differences across categories of partisan intensity. Turnout appears to be climbing only among the most partisan voters, and this trend has intensified since 2000. I argue, and the empirical analyses have implied, that these developments are attributable, at least in part, to the shifts in campaign-targeting priorities documented in Chapter 4. As such, the findings underscore that campaign strategy has important implications beyond whether candidates win or lose. Strategic decisions by campaigns affect the nature and composition of the electorate, which, as the next chapter shows, has consequences for outputs like governing and public policy.

7

WHY IS AMERICA

SO POLARIZED?

Let me now take a more comprehensive view, and warn you
in the most solemn manner, against the baneful effects of
the spirit of party generally.

—PRESIDENT GEORGE WASHINGTON,
Farewell Address (1796)

When very complicated situations collapse into simple "us
versus them" problems, then certainty, hate, and escalatory
spirals proliferate and become a driving force for perpetual
conflict.

—PETER T. COLEMAN (2011)

IT IS DIFFICULT TO IMAGINE times when America has been
as polarized along partisan or ideological lines as it is today.
Partisan polarization, which, depending on how it is measured
has been on the rise for decades, is one of the most prominent
and consequential changes in contemporary American politics
(Abramowitz and Saunders 2008). Its political consequences are
pervasive, fueling partisan conflict and legislative gridlock and
influencing policy outcomes (McCarty, Poole, and Rosenthal
2006). Widening party divergence across a range of policy areas,
including immigration, healthcare, education, and even foreign
policy, has resulted in gridlock and inaction. On some issues,
the impact of polarization has not been neutral. In the domain

Bases Loaded. Costas Panagopoulos, Oxford University Press (2021). © Oxford University Press.
DOI: 10.1093/oso/9780197533062.001.0001.

of social welfare policy, for instance, studies have shown that growing polarization has pushed redistributive policies in a conservative direction, creating disadvantages for low-income citizens and strengthening income inequality (McCarty et al. 2006; Hacker and Pierson 2010). Fowler and Hall (2016) have shown that divergence between the parties in the modern Congress does not shrink even when constituents have strong interests in a particular policy domain. Druckman, Peterson, and Slothuus (2013: 57) find "stark evidence that polarized environments fundamentally change how citizens make decisions" by intensifying the impact of party endorsements on opinions, decreasing the impact of substantive information, and stimulating greater confidence in less substantively grounded opinions.

Scholars have offered several explanations for growing polarization; some studies link polarization to changes in the media landscape (Levendusky 2013), including the (re)emergence of partisan media on cable networks and option proliferation that allows news (and politics) junkies near-constant access to viewpoints they already espouse (Prior 2007). Accessing confirmatory information or viewing like-minded partisan media has been shown to be associated with more polarized political attitudes, compared with mainstream media (Levendusky 2013; Taber and Lodge 2006). Abramowitz (2011, 2015) links polarization to growing racial and ethnic diversity in America. Altman and McDonald (2015) argue ideological polarization in Congress is affected by redistricting, specifically, the sorting of parties' incumbents into more ideologically competitive districts and the drawing of more ideologically extreme districts. Karol (2015: 68) asserts, "[p]olarization is a party story" and connects growing polarization to increased policy pressures exerted by informal networks of party activists and party-aligned interest groups seeking to pursue their narrow issue objectives.

In this chapter, I focus on whether rising partisan polarization in the United States can be linked to the shifts in presidential campaign strategy and to the corresponding changes in patterns of electoral participation documented in previous chapters. Spoiler alert: It can be. The analysis unfolds as follows. I begin with a general discussion about partisan polarization and then proceed to examine the empirical evidence connecting polarization to the changes described throughout this book. In the end, the links I observe imply changing campaign strategies over the past six decades have had profound and enduring consequences for politics and democracy in America.

PARTISAN POLARIZATION IN AMERICA

Polarization refers to divisions among individuals or groups and is viewed as movement toward extreme positions by competing forces. In American politics, partisan polarization calls attention to the growing divisions between the Democratic and Republican Parties, which have been observed at both the elite (elected officials) and mass (citizens) levels (see Theriault 2008). The severity of mass and elite polarization varies based on how it is measured and conceptualized, and scholars continue to debate how best to measure polarization at all levels. Regardless of how mass polarization is defined, strong partisans appear to have become more polarized over the last few decades, compared with weak and leaning partisans (see Lelkes 2016).

Affective polarization is one commonly used conceptualization of mass polarization. Evidence that the American public has grown more and more affectively polarized in recent years is quite strong. Affective polarization refers to the extent to which Democrats and Republicans dislike each other (Iyengar,

Sood, and Lelkes 2012). Surveys of public opinion convincingly demonstrate that the animosity between Democrats and Republicans has grown over the past few decades. Affective polarization is routinely measured using survey responses to feeling thermometers that ask respondents to place each party on a thermometer scale that ranges from 0 to 100. Respondents are informed that a placement of 50 on the scale should depict a group to which they "neither feel warm nor cold." A score greater than 50 means the individual has a "favorable or warm feeling" toward that group, whereas scores below 50 are considered to represent "cold or negative" feelings. Affective polarization scores are then calculated by subtracting the out-group ratings from the in-group scores, where the in-group is the party with which an individual identifies and the out-group is the opposition party.

Lelkes (2016) estimates that affective polarization has increased by about 8 percentage points between the late 1970s and 2012. He argues the increase in polarization is driven primarily by a decline in the out-party ratings, rather than evaluations of their own party, based on feeling thermometer ratings. In other words, partisans are rating the opposition party much more negatively than they did in the past, while maintaining a comparable rating for their party. Lelkes (2016) points out that the average ratings of one's own party were 74 and 75 in 1978 and 2012, respectively. By contrast, feeling thermometer ratings for the out-party, which averaged 47 in 1978, dropped to 30 by the 2012 election (Lelkes 2016). Some scholars assert that political campaigns are the driving force behind the growth in affective polarization among the American public, in part due to the rising exposure to negative campaign advertising in elections (Iyengar et al. 2012) that reinforces voters' partisan biases and produces a more negative outlook toward the other party (Campbell et al. 1960).

Partisans may dislike each other more today than they did forty years ago, but this does not necessarily mean the American electorate has grown further apart based on ideology or issue positions. Early studies of the American public found that only a small segment of the voting-age population could be considered "ideologues" as most people are not sufficiently informed on the issues and do not have consistent attitudes across issues or over time (Converse 1964). In fact, only a small portion of the public seemed to have a basic understanding of ideology and terms frequently associated with a concept, such as liberal and conservative (Converse 1964). These conclusions emerged from survey data collected in the 1950s, when the American citizenry was markedly less educated. Since then, the dramatic increase in education has enabled the public to think of politics increasingly in ideological terms, at least more so than their counterparts sixty years ago (Abramowitz and Saunders 2008).

Analyses of differences across a wide range of policy positions have also concluded that the public, and especially strong partisans, have become increasingly polarized over the past few decades (Abramowitz and Saunders 1998, 2008), although I note this view is not shared by all. Fiorina, Abrams, and Pope (2006), for instance, found the public may be closely but not deeply divided on issues. In other words, Americans may come down on opposing sides of issues, but only small segments feel strongly enough about them to be considered polarized. Of course, strong partisans are more likely to hold intense ideological positions. Based on ideological self-placement scores reported in surveys, Lelkes (2016) has found inconclusive evidence of ideological polarization overall, but clearer evidence that polarization has grown emerges if the analysis is restricted to partisan identifiers.

Public perceptions that polarization has grown in recent years have also intensified. Ahler (2014) reported, for example, that partisans believe that the other major political party and their supporters hold more extreme positions than they actually do on the issues (Ahler 2014). These beliefs are strongest among individuals who hold extreme positions themselves (Va Boven, Judd, and Sherman 2012). Similarly, Westfall et al. (2015) attribute these views mainly to strong partisans who believe the opposing party's supporters hold extreme positions.

Across the board, at the level of the mass electorate, most studies find strong partisans are more polarized than the rest of the electorate. These views can influence elected officials and political candidates as they contact and engage these constituencies in pursuit of victory and in governing. Alternatively, polarized voters can also elect more extreme candidates, especially in primary elections, which tend to attract disproportionate shares of more ideologically extreme voters (Panagopoulos 2010).

The influence of more polarized voters has also likely contributed to higher levels of partisan and ideological polarization at the level of the political elite. Several scholars, for example, have documented widening gaps between Democratic and Republican elected officials (Theriault 2008; McCarty et al. 2006; Poole and Rosenthal 1997). Elite polarization is commonly measured using DW-NOMINATE scores constructed for each member separately using roll call votes in Congress (Poole and Rosenthal 1997). Figure 7.1 plots the difference in DW-NOMINATE party means for the U.S. House of Representatives for each congress elected in presidential years between 1956 and 2016 (values range from 0 to 1). Higher scores indicated higher levels of partisan polarization. These scores paint a vivid picture of increased polarization along party lines in Congress, where members of each party have drifted further apart based on voting records. Following the 1956 presidential election, for the 85th Congress that was seated in 1957, the difference in party means was .55; for the

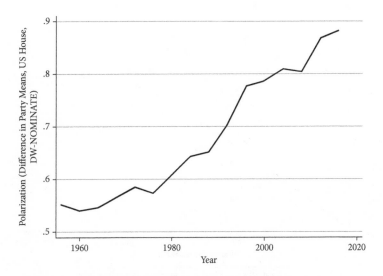

FIGURE 7.1 Partisan Polarization in the U.S. House of Representatives (Congresses Elected in Presidential Years) (1956–2016) *Source:* Voteview (Lewis et al. 2020).

115th Congress seated in 2017 after the 2016 presidential election, the corresponding figure was .88, the highest level of congressional polarization ever recorded.

Are levels of partisan polarization in Congress related to the growth in electoral participation among strong partisans described in the previous chapter? The evidence presented in Figure 7.2 (both panels) suggests this is likely the case. Panel (A) shows the correspondence between the differences in party means for congresses elected concurrently with presidential elections between 1956 and 2016 and the turnout rates among strong partisans in these cycles (as described in Chapter 6), while Panel (B) presents a parallel analysis using the turnout differential in each presidential election cycle (the difference in reported turnout rates between strong partisans and pure independents) as an alternative measure while retaining the

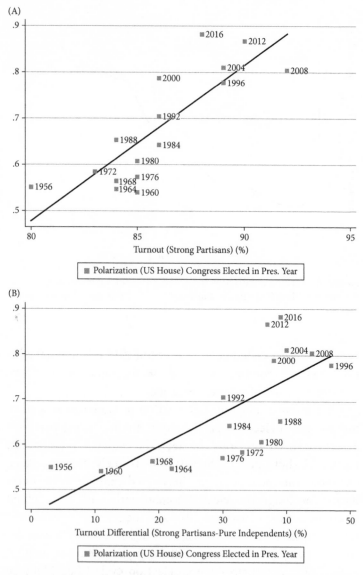

FIGURE 7.2 Partisan Polarization in the U.S. House of Representatives and Voter Turnout (1956–2016)

same polarization figures. For both sets of analyses, the positive relationship is striking and highly statistically significant. The Pearson's R correlation for data displayed in Panel (A) is .82 ($p = .0001$), and it is .73 ($p = .001$) for Panel (B). Higher levels of turnout by strong partisans, both absolute levels and relative to pure independents, are associated with greater partisan polarization in the Congress that follows. In fact, regressing the levels of House polarization on turnout rates by strong partisans in the preceding election using ordinary least squares reveals polarization grows by .03 units (standard error = .006, $p = .000$) for every 1 percentage point increase in turnout by strong partisans on average. I interpret this evidence cautiously, recognizing the causal relationships may be unclear, but the overall story is consistent with the claim that heightened influence likely exerted by an ever-increasing share of base partisans in the electorate, relative to more moderate, independent, or persuadable voters, manifests as growing levels of political polarization.

In a final set of analyses, I use ordinary least squares (OLS) regression to explain partisan polarization in the U.S. House as a function of time using a year counter. I also investigate whether there were any enduring shifts in partisan polarization that can be traced to the 2000 election cycle and its aftermath by adding a dichotomous indicator to denote elections before and since (and including) 2000. The results confirm partisan polarization has grown significantly over this period. The coefficient for the time trend equals .02 (standard error = .002, $p = .000$, two-tailed). The analyses also reveal the indicator for elections starting in 2000 is positive (coefficient = .05, standard error = .025) and statistically significant at the $p = .07$ level (two-tailed), confirming, as expected, that the long-term trend of growing partisan polarization in Congress has accelerated since 2000.

CONCLUSION

Some observers are not deeply troubled by current levels of polarization in America. Campbell (2016: 219) notes, for example, "as unpleasant and contentious as it often becomes, party polarization of some degree is a natural characteristic of competitive democratic party politics." For those who express greater concern about deepening divides in American politics, however, understanding the various sources of the phenomenon is crucial. In my view, there exists an electoral dimension to partisan polarization that, in all likelihood, is intensifying. The analyses presented in this chapter suggest that patterns of growing partisan polarization, at least as measured by roll call votes taken in the U.S. House of Representatives in Congress, are linked to patterns of electoral participation. If it is the case, as I have argued, that campaign strategies influence the kinds of voters who are targeted, which in turn affects the composition of the electorate on Election Day, then it is reasonable to conclude that at least part of the heightened level of polarization characterizing the political reality in America today can be traced back to campaign activities. These findings underscore the notion that what campaigns do matters—not only for election outcomes, but also for the nature of political processes in the United States and for American democracy more broadly.

8

CONCLUSION

Our party, like any other political party, strives for political supremacy *for itself.*

—VLADIMIR LENIN

If candidates are campaigning primarily by speaking to like-minded constituents, why would we expect them to govern any differently?

—TODD AND DANN (2017)

CAMPAIGNS ARE LIKE WARS. THE ways campaigns are waged are consequential, and the election outcomes they help secure can have significant and long-lasting effects, shaping politics and policies in democratic polities for long periods. Yet while political campaigns can give rise to important consequences for democracy, their primary motivation is to win elections (Panagopoulos 2017). Considerations for wider impact on democracy and the political system *writ large* are likely secondary or tangential as best. New and emerging technologies make it easier for political campaigns to pursue these goals, but that does not necessarily translate into positive developments for American politics and society.

The stakes are high. Opinion polls suggest large majorities of the American public are dissatisfied with the political system and believe it requires wholesale or fundamental change (Panagopoulos and Weinschenk 2015). Many Americans are frustrated with the hyperpolarized political climate, with gridlock and dysfunction, and with the lack of responsiveness to

Bases Loaded. Costas Panagopoulos, Oxford University Press (2021). © Oxford University Press.
DOI: 10.1093/oso/9780197533062.001.0001.

their needs. Hopeless, some have given up entirely and withdrawn from politics altogether. With few incentives to reengage them and to bring them back into the fold, the political process has essentially abandoned them.

Political campaigns bear some responsibility for these developments. Over the course of the past six decades, political campaigns have turned their eyes increasingly toward the base, including coalitions of party activists, and dampening the influence of scores of citizens, including more centrist and moderate voices, in electoral discourse and participation. Elections in early twenty-first-century America have become primarily battles of the bases. As Todd and Dann (2017) observe, "[t]hanks to the assumption now among too many political strategists that the easiest and best path to victory is to search for like-minded voters, both parties have essentially stopped courting the vacillating middle entirely." "The result," argue Todd and Dann (2017), "is today's crisis of governing, with the halls of Congress populated by lawmakers who feel beholden not to all their constituents, but only to their supporters." At the presidential level, Donald Trump appears to have been catapulted to the White House in large part by focusing on his base supporters on Twitter (and other digital platforms that facilitate direct outreach), prompting analysts to ponder whether Trump's approach "may signal a shift in presidential rhetorical strategy from an address of a wide constituency (built on coalitions) to a core constituency (built on a base)" (Stolee and Caton 2018: 164). Some observers have argued that Trump's overwhelming attentiveness to the GOP base extended well into the governing domain and became a hallmark of his administration. One commentator, who described Trump's focus on his base as "monomaniacal," observed that, "Trump has governed with the same divisive dystopianism that marked his campaign, loudly narrowcasting to his most ardent supporters with little apparent regard for who else hears him" (Schlesinger

2019). "It's a symbiotic relationship," Schlesinger (2019) continued, "Trump revels in his supporters' adulation, while they bask in the fact that when he speaks it's to them and them alone." On the other side of the political aisle, strong showings by self-proclaimed "revolutionary" and "Democratic Socialist" Vermont senator Bernie Sanders in both the 2016 and 2020 Democratic primary contests are a testament to the triumph of the progressive base and its growing influence, especially in primary elections, which attract disproportionately more extreme partisans (Panagopoulos 2010).

A common refrain by political candidates on the campaign trail is that every vote matters. But that is not exactly true. For most political contenders, the votes they care about are the votes that will shore up their tallies on Election Day. These are the votes they covet and cultivate, largely—and increasingly—ignoring many others.

For their part, citizens are not completely blameless. Firmly entrenched in their ideological camps, many Americans succumb to confirmation bias, seeking solace in media echo chambers and political silos that only ossify their partisan views (Arceneaux and Johnson 2013; Jamieson and Cappella 2008). Resistance to opposing viewpoints can be almost visceral (Zaller 1992). Still others, fearing ostracism and rejection for unpopular views, spiral into silence (Noelle-Neumann 1993). Many voters treat politics as sport, rationalizing their political choices (Lodge and Taber 2013) and rooting for their side to win at almost any cost, impervious to any other considerations (Mason 2018). Social identities constructed around partisan identification leave little room to embrace out-group members (Green, Palmquist, and Schickler 2002; Mason 2018; Walsh 2004). Even when Democrats and Republicans agree on policy outcomes, the distrust and social divisions between them prevent unity and cooperation (Mason 2018). Political compromise is too infrequently rewarded, while moderation is too often punished.

Perhaps worse yet, far too many citizens are politically discon-
nected and disengaged.

Some division can be expected, and may be completely
natural, if, as Hibbing, Smith, and Alford (2014) have argued,
individuals are genetically predisposed to distinct ideological outlooks. At the level of the political elite, Grossman and
Hopkins (2016) have shown that Democrats and Republicans
perceive politics differently, rely on distinct sources of information, argue past one another, and pursue divergent goals in
government. The authors assert there is an asymmetry in the
party system, with Republican leaders prizing conservatism
and attracting support by pledging loyalty to broad values and
Democratic leaders seeking concrete government action by
appealing to voters' group identities and interests by endorsing
specific policies (Grossman and Hopkins 2016). Grossman and
Hopkins (2016) view the Republican Party as the vehicle of an
ideological movement and the Democratic Party as a coalition
of social groups, and these differences mire contemporary politics in polarization and governing dysfunction. Egan (2013)
argues different issue priorities across the two major parties dis-
tort American politics further. The studies suggest differences
between Democrats and Republicans, at both the mass and elite
levels, are deeply rooted, enduring features that foster biases
that are difficult—but not impossible—to overcome.

In presidential elections, institutional arrangements also
create imbalances and inequities with broad implications for
democracy. The Electoral College system, coupled with the
winner-take-all allocation of electoral votes in all states but
two (Maine and Nebraska), focuses competition on a relatively
small subset of battleground states (Shaw 2006). Despite the
balanced nature of presidential voting in these states, it is interesting to note that partisan identification is distributed similarly in battleground and non-battleground states. In 2016, for
example, 37 percent of voters in battleground states identified

as strong partisans (19 percent as strong Democrats and 17 percent as strong Republicans) compared with 39 percent in non-battleground states (23 percent as strong Democrats and 16 percent as strong Republicans). The shares of pure independents in battleground and non-battleground states in 2016 were virtually identical (14 and 15 percent respectively). Regardless, voters in uncompetitive states are virtually ignored by national, presidential campaigns seeking to maximize resources, often neglecting majorities of Americans. Overlooked and under-mobilized, smaller shares of eligible voters in these states cast ballots on Election Day (Bergan et al. 2005).

Majority of Americans also tell public opinion researchers that they prefer leaders who compromise to get things done. In 2019, a Pew Research Center study found that 65 percent of Americans believed it was "very important that elected officials be willing to make compromises with their opponents to solve important problems," but it was mainly the opposing party that respondents wanted to see make the compromises (Tyson 2019). Given these circumstances, it is unsurprising that voters keep electing politicians who refuse to compromise (Bond, Fleisher, and Cohen 2015). As Bond et al. (2015: 149) caution, "[g]ridlock is likely to remain until the voters start voting for the type of leaders that they say they want."

If citizens, then, are part of the problem, they are almost certainly part of the solution. Voters can force campaigns to take notice by becoming active and engaged. As I have noted throughout this book, political campaigns go where the votes are, where the fish are. Many Americans must get back in game and put pressure on political candidates and campaigns to win them over on substance, not on gimmicks, cheap tricks, or superficial platitudes imbedded in thirty-second ads or speeches at campaign rallies. Campaigns must give voters good reasons to vote for them above and beyond simply shared partisanship, and voters may need to put their party biases aside and extend their considerations of candidate qualifications beyond party labels.

Even the digital big data revolution, which "[f]or all its complexity . . . has flattened our political campaigns into 1s and 0s," according to Todd and Dann (2017), can be harnessed for good. "A rethinking of how we use Big Data in our politics could go a long way in fixing what is clearly a disease of governing dysfunction," assert Todd and Dann (2017), adding, "[b]y all means, let's use all the digital power and data in the world to communicate, to analyze, to organize, to educate."

To some extent, there is a chicken or egg dimension to this discussion. Which comes first? Who is responsive to whom? Are voters responsive to campaigns, or are campaigns responsive to voters? Resolving this debate is beyond the scope of this book, but it is likely a bit of both. At least to some degree, these processes are mutually reinforcing, working in tandem and in symbiotic ways.

It is clear that some of the trends described throughout this book have troubling implications, but it is important not to lose sight of encouraging signs. First, it is clear that parties are not neglecting less committed sympathizers altogether in their targeting efforts. Persuasion is not completely dead in presidential campaigns. In fact, the evidence described in this book shows that both parties' outreach to independent voters and even cross-partisans seems to have grown markedly, in absolute terms, over the period I investigated. This finding implies both major parties remain actively and increasingly engaged in at least some persuasion efforts in presidential elections. My analyses simply reflect base supporters are attracting greater and greater attention from their respective partisan camps relative to other voters. That said, the patterns detected in this book are likely tentative and subject to change and fluctuation as parties and campaigns continue to adapt to ever-changing sociopolitical and contextual circumstances. Furthermore, some of the trends I describe are based on just a few election cycles, and there are hints that some things may already be shifting. Reinforcement, stability, or reversals in the patterns I identify are entirely conceivable. I concede further that the evidence presented is mainly observational and, as such, largely speculative and suggestive, not subject to causal interpretation. So while I hesitate to extract too much from the results, I do not dismiss them. Scholars will need to be vigilant in monitoring developments in successive cycles to determine whether these patterns—and their implications—are reinforced or abandoned.

APPENDIX

Table A1

TECHNICAL SPECIFICATION (LOGISTIC REGRESSION) CORRESPONDING TO FIGURE 4.5

	Time-Trend
Partisanship	−4.320**
	(1.347)
Year	0.011***
	(0.001)
Interaction: Partisanship * Year	0.002***
	(0.001)
Constant	−23.944***
	(2.969)
Num. obs.	31015

*** signifies statistical significance at the $p < 0.001$ level, ** at the $p < 0.01$ level, and * at the $p < 0.05$ level using two-tailed tests. All models use probabilistic survey weights.

Table A2

TECHNICAL SPECIFICATION (LOGISTIC REGRESSION) CORRESPONDING TO FIGURE 4.6 (PANEL A)

	Trend With Post-2000 Change
Partisanship	**−8.185****
	(2.669)
Year	**−0.009****
	(0.003)
Interaction: Partisanship * Year	**0.004****
	(0.001)
Post-2000	**0.838*****
	(0.112)
Interaction: Partisanship * Post-2000	−0.061
	(0.052)
Constant	**15.480****
	(5.876)
Num. obs.	31015

*** signifies statistical significance at the $p < 0.001$ level, ** at the $p < 0.01$ level, and * at the $p<0.05$ level using two-tailed tests. All models use probabilistic survey weights.

TECHNICAL SPECIFICATION (LOGISTIC REGRESSION) CORRESPONDING TO FIGURE 4.6 (PANEL B)

	Trend with Extended Demographics
Partisanship	**−6.732***
	(2.749)
Year	**−0.009****
	(0.003)
Interaction: Partisanship * Year	**0.003***
	(0.001)
Post-2000	**0.819*****
	(0.116)
Interaction: Partisanship *	−0.039
Post-2000	(0.054)
Age	**0.018*****
	(0.001)
Female	0.000
	(0.026)
Race: Black	**−0.139****
	(0.045)
Race: Hispanic	**−0.350*****
	(0.057)
Race: Other Non-White	**−0.344*****
	(0.078)
Education	**0.500*****
	(0.028)
Union	**0.255*****
	(0.033)
Never Married	**−0.229*****
	(0.041)
Religion: Protestant	−0.035
	(0.088)
Religion: Catholic	0.050
	(0.090)
Religion: Other Non-Christian	**−0.192***
	(0.092)
Constant	**14.709***
	(6.097)
Num. obs.	30176

*** signifies statistical significance at the $p<0.001$ level, ** at the $p<0.01$ level, and * at the $p<0.05$ level using two-tailed tests. All models use probabilistic survey weights.

TECHNICAL SPECIFICATION (LOGISTIC REGRESSION) CORRESPONDING TO FIGURE 4.8

	Republicans	*Democrats*
Partisanship	−1.827	**4.944*****
	(1.463)	(1.472)
Year	**−0.010****	**0.008***
	(0.003)	(0.003)
Interaction: Partisanship * Year	0.001	**−0.003*****
	(0.001)	(0.001)
Post-2000	**0.895*****	**0.863*****
	(0.138)	(0.119)
Interaction: Partisanship * Post-2000	0.000	−0.011
	(0.030)	(0.030)
Age	**0.021*****	**0.017*****
	(0.001)	(0.001)
Female	−0.040	−0.018
	(0.031)	(0.030)
Race: Black	**−0.534*****	−0.001
	(0.064)	(0.050)
Race: Hispanic	**−0.580*****	**−0.281*****
	(0.076)	(0.064)
Race: Other Non-White	**−0.478*****	**−0.243****
	(0.096)	(0.085)
Education	**0.502*****	**0.440*****
	(0.033)	(0.032)
Union	**0.167*****	**0.310*****
	(0.039)	(0.037)
Never Married	**−0.307*****	**−0.191*****
	(0.051)	(0.046)
Religion: Protestant	0.164	−0.167
	(0.107)	(0.096)
Religion: Catholic	0.196	−0.005
	(0.109)	(0.098)
Religion: Other Non-Christian	−0.184	**−0.256***
	(0.112)	(0.100)
Constant	**16.357***	**−17.352****
	(6.800)	(6.028)
Num. obs.	29889	29889

*** signifies statistical significance at the $p<0.001$ level, ** at the $p<0.01$ level, and * at the $p<0.05$ level using two-tailed tests. All models use probabilistic survey weights.

Table A5

TECHNICAL SPECIFICATION (LOGISTIC REGRESSION) CORRESPONDING TO FIGURE 6.6

	Trend With Post-2000
Partisan Intensity	−**12.477*****
	(1.349)
Year	−**0.016*****
	(0.002)
Interaction: Intensity * Year	**0.007*****
	(0.001)
Post-2000 Indicator	**0.331*****
	(0.052)
Constant	**31.154*****
	(3.588)
Num. obs.	32417

*** signifies statistical significance at the $p<0.001$ level, ** at the $p<0.01$ level and * at the $p<0.05$ leveal using two-tailed tests. All models use probabilistic survey weights.

NOTES

Chapter 1

1. For analyses using ANES throughout, I use the ANES Time Series Cumulative Data File version released on September 10, 2019. Unless otherwise noted, analyses are based on combined (face-to-face and web/Internet modes) samples and weighted accordingly. Details available upon request.

Chapter 3

1. The author is grateful to Kyle Endres who compiled and shared these data.
2. For 2008 and 2012, the ANES did not code responses to many of the open-ended questions. Coding for these years was done by the author.

Chapter 4

1. To address this concern more directly, I replicate the key analyses using fixed-year effects to capture any election cycle-specific effects on contact reports or recollections. The analyses reveal no substantive changes to the results. Details available upon request.

2. These proportions are calculated using probabilistic survey weights that increase or decrease the statistical weight associated with each individual respondent so that the full sample is more accurately representative of the U.S. population in that year. The analyses reported throughout apply weights accordingly, unless otherwise indicated. Unweighted analyses yield substantively similar results. I do not report unweighted results but can provide these upon request.

3. These tests were conducted using the *estat sbsingle* post-estimation command in Stata 16. Details available upon request.

4. Substantively similar conclusions can be drawn from the alternative average Wald and average likelihood-ratio tests that can reject the bull hypothesis of no break at the $p = .0702$ and $p = .0621$ levels respectively.

5. Although I note the supremum Wald statistic is 7.9866, $p = .206$, is statistically insignificant at conventional levels, the alternative, average Wald and average likelihood-ratio tests are statistically significant at the $p = .064$ and $p = .045$, respectively, implying the null hypothesis of no structural break can be rejected.

6. Supremum Wald statistic = 29.986, $p = .000$; average Wald statistic = 6.392, $p = .014$; average LR test statistic = 5.690, $p = .022$.

7. Shaded areas in figures represent 95% confidence intervals.

8. Coded dichotomously such that "married/separated/widowed/partner" equals 1, and "never married" is 0.

Chapter 5

1. The author is grateful to Travis Ridout for generously providing the 2012 and 2016 data used for these analyses (personal correspondence). Data for the 2000, 2004, and 2008 cycles was obtained by the author from the Wisconsin Advertising Project.

2. The author is grateful to Darrell West for generously providing the data used for these analyses. Personal correspondence.

Chapter 6

1. Source: http://www.electproject.org/national-1789-present.

BIBLIOGRAPHY

Abramowitz, A. (2011). *The disappearing center: Engaged citizens, polarization, and American democracy.* Yale University Press.

Abramowitz, A. I. (2015). The New American Electorate. In J. Thurber and A. Yoshinaka (Eds.), *American gridlock: The sources, character and impact of political polarization.* Cambridge University Press (pp. 19–44).

Abramowitz, A. I., and Saunders, K. L. (1998). Ideological realignment in the U.S. electorate. *Journal of Politics, 60*(3), 634–652.

Abramowitz, A. I., and Saunders, K. L. (2008). Is polarization a myth? *Journal of Politics, 70*(2), 542–555.

Abramson, P. R., Aldrich, J. H., and Rohde, D. W. (2002). *Change and continuity in the 2000 elections.* CQ Press.

Ahler, D. J. (2014). Self-fulfilling misperceptions of public polarization. *Journal of Politics, 76*(3), 607–620.

Aldrich, J. H. (1995). *Why parties?: The origin and transformation of political parties in America.* University of Chicago Press.

Aldrich, J. H. (1993). Rational choice and turnout. *American Journal of Political Science, 37*(1): 246–278.

Altman, M., and McDonald, M. (2015). Redistricting and polarization. In J. Thurber and A. Yoshinaka (Eds.), *American gridlock: The sources, character and impact of political polarization.* Cambridge University Press. (pp. 45–67).

Ambinder, M. (2009, October 5). Exclusive: How the Democrats won the data war in 2008. *The Atlantic*. Accessed online October 9, 2019: https://www.theatlantic.com/politics/archive/2009/10/exclusive-how-democrats-won-the-data-war-in-2008/27647/.

American National Election Studies Time Series Cumulative Data File [data set]. Stanford University and the University of Michigan. Released September 10, 2019.

Ansolabehere, S., and Iyengar, S. (1995). *Going negative: How attack ads shrink and polarize the electorate*. Free Press.

Arceneaux, K., and Johnson, M. (2013). *Changing minds or changing channels: Partisan news in an age of choice*. University of Chicago Press.

Bailey, M. A., Hopkins, D. J., and Rogers, T. (2016). Unresponsive and unpersuaded: The unintended consequences of a voter persuasion effort. *Political Behavior*, 38(3), 713–746.

Baker, P. (2014). *Days of fire: Bush and Cheney in the White House*. Anchor Books.

Balz, D. (2006, October 28) Democrats aim to regain edge in getting voters to the polls. *Washington Post*. Accessed online November 7, 2019: https://www.washingtonpost.com/wp-dyn/content/article/2006/10/07/AR2006100700388.html.

Bartels, L. M. (1993). Messages received: The political impact of media exposure. *American Political Science Review*, 87(2), 267–285.

Beck, P. A., and Heidemann, E. D. (2014). Changing strategies in grassroots canvassing: 1956–2012. *Party Politics*, 20(2), 261–274.

Berelson, B., Lazarsfeld, P., and McPhee, W. (1954). *Voting: A study of opinion formation in a presidential campaign*. University of Chicago Press.

Bergan, D., Gerber, A. S., Green, D. P., and Panagopoulos, C. (2005). Grassroots mobilization and voter turnout in 2004. *Public Opinion Quarterly* 69(5): 760–777.

Bishop, B. (2009). *The big sort: Why the clustering of like-minded America is tearing us apart*. Houghton Mifflin Harcourt.

Blais, A. (2000). *To vote or not to vote?: The merits and limits of rational choice theory*. University of Pittsburgh Press.

Bond, J., Fleisher, R., and Cohen, J. (2015). Presidential-congressional relations in an era of polarized parties and a 60-vote Senate. In J. Thurber and A. Yoshinaka (Eds.), *American gridlock: The sources, character and impact of political polarization.* Cambridge University Press. (pp. 133–151).

Brady, H. E., Verba, S., and Schlozman, K. L. (1995). Beyond SES: A resource model of political participation. *American Political Science Review, 89*(2), 271–294.

Brambor, T., Clark, W. R., and Golder, M. (2006). Understanding interaction models: Improving empirical analyses. *Political Analysis, 14*(1), 63–82.

Burton, M. J., Miller, W. J., and Shea, D. (2015). *Campaign craft: The strategies, tactics, and art of political campaign management.* 5th ed. ABC-CLIO.

Campbell, A., Converse, P. E., Miller, W. E., and Stokes, D. E. (1960). *The American voter.* John Wiley and Sons.

Campbell, J. (2016). *Polarized: making sense of a divided America.* Princeton University Press.

Cohen, J. E. (1999). Examined lives: Informational privacy and the subject as object. *Stanford Law Review, 52*: 1373–1438.

Cohen, J. E. (2000). Examined lives: Informational privacy and the subject as object. *Georgetown Law Faculty Publications and Other Works.* 810.

Coleman, P. T. (2011). *The five percent: Finding solutions to seemingly impossible conflicts.* Public Affairs.

Condon, M., Larimer C. W., and Panagopoulos, C. (2016). Partisan social pressure and voter mobilization. *American Politics Research, 44*(6), 982–1007.

Converse, P. E. (1964). The nature of belief systems in mass publics. In D.E. Apter (ed.) *Ideology and Its Discontent.* New York: Free Press of Glencoe. (pp. 206–261).

Cox, G. W. (1999). Electoral rules and the calculus of mobilization. *Legislative Studies Quarterly, 24*(3), 387–419.

Davies, H. (2015, December 11). Ted Cruz using firm that harvested data on millions of unwitting Facebook users. *The Guardian.* Accessed online January 20, 2020: https://www.theguardian.com/us-news/2015/dec/11/senator-ted-cruz-president-campaign-facebook-user-data.

Dehay, P. (2016, December 30). Microtargeting of low-information voters. *Medium.com.* Accessed online October 9, 2019: https://medium.com/personaldata-io/microtargeting-of-low-information-voters-6eb2520cd473.

Dimock, M., Clark, A., and Horowitz, J. M. (2008). Campaign dynamics and the swing vote in the 2004 election. In W. G. Mayer (Ed.), *The Swing Voter in American Politics*. Brookings Institution Press. (pp. 58–74).

Downs, A. (1957). *An economic theory of democracy*. Addison–Wesley.

Dreazen, Y. (2006: October 31). Democrats, playing catch-up, tap database to woo potential voters. *The Wall Street Journal*, A1.

Druckman, J. N., Peterson, E., and Slothuus, R. (2013). How elite partisan polarization affects public opinion formation. *American Political Science Review, 107*(1), 57–79.

Egan, P. J. (2013). *Partisan priorities: How issue ownership drives and distorts American politics*. Cambridge University Press.

eMarketer. (2020, February 12). U.S. political ad spending to hit record high. https://www.emarketer.com/newsroom/index.php/us-political-ad-spending-to-hit-record-high/.

Endres, K. (2016). Issue cross-pressures and campaign effects: Connecting the right voters with the right message. Ph.D. Dissertation, University of Texas at Austin.

Enos, R., Fowler, A., and Vavreck, L. (2014). Increasing Inequality: The effect of GOTV mobilization on the composition of the electorate. *Journal of Politics 76*(1): 273–288.

Erikson, R., Panagopoulos, C., and Wlezien, C. (2010). The crystallization of voter preferences during the 2008 presidential campaign. *Presidential Studies Quarterly 40*(3): 482–496.

Erikson, R., and Wlezien, C. (2012). *The timeline of presidential elections: How campaigns do (and do not) matter*. University of Chicago Press.

Fiorina, M. P., Abrams, S. J., and Pope, J. C. (2006). *Culture war? The myth of a polarized America*. 2nd ed. Pearson Longman.

Fiske, S., and Taylor, S. (1984). *Social cognition*. 2nd ed. McGraw-Hill.

Flanigan, W., Zingale, N., Theisse-Morse, E., and Wagner, M. (2015). *Political behavior of the American electorate*. 13th ed. Sage.

Foos, F., and de Rooji, E. A. (2017). The role of partisan cues in voter mobilization campaigns: Evidence from a randomized field experiment. *Electoral Studies 45*: 63–74.

Fowler, A., and Hall, A. (2016). The elusive quest for convergence. *Quarterly Journal of Political Science, 11*: 131–149.

Fowler, E. F., and Ridout, T. N. (2013). Negative, angry, and ubiquitous: Political advertising in 2012. *The Forum, 10*(4): 51–61. De Gruyter.

Franke-Ruta, G. (2004, January 15). The GOP deploys. *The American Prospect*. Accessed online March 1, 2020: https://prospect.org/features/gop-deploys/.

Franz, M. M., Fowler, E. F., Ridout, T., and Wang, M. Y. (2020). The issue focus of online and television advertising in the 2016 presidential campaign. *American Politics Research, 48*(1), 175–196.

Franz, M. M., and Ridout, T. N. (2007). Does political advertising persuade? *Political Behavior, 29*(4), 465–491.

Freedman, P., Franz, M., and Goldstein, K. (2004). Campaign advertising and democratic citizenship. *American Journal of Political Science, 48*(4), 723–741.

Frontline. (2005, January 4). Interview with Matthew Dowd. Accessed online April 3, 2019: https://www.pbs.org/wgbh/pages/frontline/shows/architect/interviews/dowd.html.

Fung, B., Timberg, C., and Gold, M. (2017, June 19). A republican contractor's database of nearly every voter was left exposed on the internet for 12 days, researcher says. *Wall Street Journal*. Accessed online March 1, 2020: https://www.washingtonpost.com/news/the-switch/wp/2017/06/19/republican-contractor-database-every-voter-exposed-internet-12-days-researcher-says/

Gardner, J. A. (2009). *What are campaigns for?: The role of persuasion in electoral law and politics.* Oxford University Press.

Geer, J. G. (2006). *In defense of negativity: Attack ads in presidential campaigns.* University of Chicago Press.

Geer, J. G. (2008). *In defense of negativity: Attack ads in presidential campaigns.* University of Chicago Press.

Gerber, A. S., Gimpel, J. G., Green, D. P., and Shaw, D. R. (2011). How large and long-lasting are the persuasive effects of televised campaign ads? Results from a randomized field experiment. *American Political Science Review, 105*(1), 135–150.

Gerber, A. S., and Green, D. P. (2000). The effects of canvassing, telephone calls, and direct mail on voter turnout: A field experiment. *American Political Science Review, 94*(3), 653–663.

Gerber, A. S., Green, D. P., and Larimer, C. W. (2008) "Social pressure and voter turnout: Evidence from a large-scale field experiment." *American Political Science Review, 102*(1): 33–48.

Gerber, A. S., Green, D. P., and Larimer, C. W. (2010). An experiment testing the relative effectiveness of encouraging voter participation by inducing feelings of pride or shame. *Political Behavior, 32*(3), 409–422.

Gibbs, S. (2016, March 7). How did email grow from messages between academics to a global epidemic? *The Guardian.* Accessed online March 1, 2020: https://www.theguardian.com/technology/2016/mar/07/email-ray-tomlinson-history.

Goldstein, A. (2004, August 6). Bush talks jobs issues in swing states. *Washington Post,* A6.

Green, D. P., and Gerber, A. S. (2012). *Get out the vote: How to increase voter turnout.* 3rd ed. Brookings Institution.

Green, D. P., Gerber, A. S., and Nickerson, D. W. (2003). Getting out the vote in local elections: Results from six door-to-door canvassing experiments. *Journal of Politics, 65*(4), 1083–1096.

Green, D. P., Palmquist, B., and Schickler, E. (2002). *Partisan hearts and minds: Political parties and the social identities of voters.* Yale University Press.

Grossman, M., and Hopkins, D. (2016). *Asymmetric politics: Ideological Republicans and group interest Democrats.* Oxford University Press.

Hacker, J., and Pierson, P. (2010). Winner-take-all politics: Public policy, political organization, and the precipitous rise of top incomes in the United States. *Politics and Society, 38*(2): 152–204.

Hamilton, J. T. (2005). *The market and the media.* New York: Oxford University Press.

Hersh, E. D. (2015). *Hacking the electorate: How campaigns perceive voters.* Cambridge University Press.

Hersh, E. D., and Schaffner, B. F. (2013). Targeted campaign appeals and the value of ambiguity. *Journal of Politics, 75*(2), 520–534.

Hetherington, M. J. (2001). Resurgent mass partisanship: The role of elite polarization. *American Political Science Review, 95*(3), 619–631.

Hibberd, J. (2014, November 3). Favorite TV shows of Republicans vs. Democrats. *Entertainment Weekly.* Accessed online March 3, 2019: https://ew.com/article/2014/11/03/republican-democrats-favorite-tv-shows/.

Hibbing, J. R., Smith, K. B., and Alford, J. A. (2014) *Predisposed: Liberal, conservatives and the biology of political differences.* Routledge.

Hillygus, D. S., and Shields, T. G. (2008). *The persuadable voter: Wedge issues in presidential campaigns*. Princeton University Press.

Holian, D. B. (2004). He's stealing my issues! Clinton's crime rhetoric and the dynamics of issue ownership. *Political Behavior, 26*(2), 95–124.

Hovland, C. I. (1959). Reconciling conflicting results derived from experimental and survey studies of attitude change. *American Psychologist, 14*(1), 8.

Howard, P. N. (2006). *New media campaigns and the managed citizen*. Cambridge University Press.

Huckfeldt, R., and Sprague, J. (1992). Political parties and electoral mobilization: Political structure, social structure, and the party canvass. *American Political Science Review, 86*(1), 70–86.

Issenberg, S. (2012). *The victory lab: The secret science of winning campaigns*. Broadway Books.

Iyengar, S., and Hahn, K. S. (2009). Red media, blue media: Evidence of ideological selectivity in media use. *Journal of Communication, 59*(1), 19–39.

Iyengar, S., Sood, G., and Lelkes, Y. (2012). Affect, not ideology: A social identity perspective on polarization. *Public Opinion Quarterly, 76*(3), 405–431.

Jamieson, K. H. (1996). *Packaging the presidency: A history and criticism of presidential campaign advertising*. 3rd ed. Oxford University Press.

Jamieson, K. H., and Cappella, J. N. (2008). *Echo chamber: Rush Limbaugh and the conservative media establishment*. Oxford University Press.

Jones, J. M. (2008). Swing voters in the Gallup poll, 1944 to 2004. In W. G. Mayer (Ed.), *The swing voter in American politics*. Brookings Institution Press (pp. 32–57).

Kalla, J., and Broockman, D. (2018). The minimal persuasive effects of campaign contact in general elections: Evidence from 49 experiments. *American Political Science Review 112*(1), 148–166.

Karol, D. (2015). Party activists, interest groups and polarization in American politics. In J. Thurber and A. Yoshinaka (Eds.), *American gridlock: The sources, character and impact of political polarization*. Cambridge University Press. (pp. 68–85).

Kasanoff, B., Rogers, M., and Peppers, D. (2001). *Making it personal: How to profit from personalization without invading privacy.* Perseus.

Kessel, J. (1992). *Presidential campaign politics.* 4th ed. Brooks/Cole.

Key, V. O. (1966). *The responsible electorate.* Harvard University Press.

Kizza, J. M. (2013). *Ethical and social issues in the information age.* 5th ed. Springer Press.

Klapper, J. T. (1960). *The effects of mass communication.* Free Press.

Kornblut, A. (2004, August 30). Strategist focuses on president's devotees. *Boston Globe.* Accessed online May 1, 2019: http://archive.boston.com/news/nation/articles/2004/08/30/strategist_focuses_on_presidents_devotees/.

Kozlowki, M. (2019, September 18). Is Big Data Corrupting the U.S. Election Process? *Center for Digital Ethics and Policy.* Accessed online March 1, 2020 at: https://www.digitalethics.org/essays/big-data-corrupting-us-election-process

Krasno, J. S., and Green, D. P. (2008). Do televised presidential ads increase voter turnout? Evidence from a natural experiment. *Journal of Politics, 70*(1), 245–261.

Krosnick, J. A., and Kinder, D. R. (1990). Altering the foundations of support for the president through priming. *American Political Science Review, 84*(2), 497–512.

Krupnikov, Y. (2011). When does negativity demobilize? Tracing the conditional effect of negative campaigning on voter turnout. *American Journal of Political Science, 55*(4), 797–813.

Krupnikov, Y. (2014). How negativity can increase and decrease voter turnout: The effect of timing. *Political Communication, 31*(3), 446–466.

Lawrence, D. (2001). On the resurgence of party identification in the 1990s. In J. Cohen, R. Fleisher, and P. Kantor (Eds.). *American political parties: Decline or resurgence?* CQ Press.

Layman, G. C., and Carsey, T. M. (2002). Party polarization and "conflict extension" in the American electorate. *American Journal of Political Science, 46*(4), 786–802.

Lazarsfeld, P., Berelson, B., and Gaudet, B. (1944). *The people's choice: How the voter makes up his mind in a presidential campaign.* Columbia University Press.

Lelkes, Y. (2016). Mass polarization: Manifestations and measurements. *Public Opinion Quarterly, 80*(S1), 392–410.

Levendusky, M. (2009). *The partisan sort: How liberals became Democrats and conservatives became Republicans*. University of Chicago Press.

Levendusky, M. (2013). *How partisan media polarize America*. University of Chicago Press.

Lewis, J. B., Poole, K., Rosenthal, H., Boche, A., Rudkin, A., and Sonnet, L. (2020). Voteview: Congressional Roll-Call Votes Database. https://voteview.com/.

Lewis, P., and P. Hilder. (2018, March 23). Leaked: Cambridge Analytica's blueprint for Trump victory. *The Guardian*. Accessed online October 10, 2019: https://www.theguardian.com/uk-news/2018/mar/23/leaked-cambridge-analyticas-blueprint-for-trump-victory.

Lodge, M., and Taber, C. S. (2013). *The rationalizing voter*. Cambridge University Press.

Lovett, M. J., and Peress, M. (2010). *Targeting political advertising on television*. Simon Graduate School of Business, University of Rochester.

Lupia, A. (1994). Shortcuts versus encyclopedias: Information and voting behavior in California insurance reform elections. *American Political Science Review 88*(1), 63–76.

Magleby, D. B. (Ed.). (2002). *Financing the 2000 elections*. Brookings Institution Press.

Malchow, H. (2003). *The new political targeting*. Washington, DC, Campaigns and Elections.

Mann, R. (2011). *Daisy petals and mushroom clouds: LBJ, Barry Goldwater, and the ad that changed American politics*. Louisiana State University Press.

Mason, L. (2018). *Uncivil agreement: How politics became our identity*. University of Chicago Press.

Mattes, K., and Redlawsk, D. P. (2014). *The positive case for negative campaigning*. University of Chicago Press.

Mayer, W. (2007). The swing voter in American presidential elections. *American Politics Research 35*(3): 358–88.

McCarty, N. M., Poole, K. T., and Rosenthal, H. (1997). *Income redistribution and the realignment of American politics*. American Enterprise Institute Press.

McCarty, N., Poole, K. T., and Rosenthal, H. (2006). *Polarized America: The dance of ideology and unequal riches*. MIT Press.

McClurg, S.D., and Habel, P.(2011). Presidential elections: Campaigning within a segmented electorate. In S. Medvic (Ed.), *New Directions in Campaigns and Elections*. Routledge Press. (pp. 200–220).

McDonald, M. P. (2003). On the overreport bias of the National Election Study turnout rate. *Political Analysis, 11*(2), 180–186.

McDonald, M. P. (2016). Voter turnout. *United States Elections Project*. Accessed online March 1, 2018: http://www.electproject.org/home/voter-turnout/voter-turnout-data.

Miller, W. E. (1991). Party identification, realignment, and party voting: Back to the basics. *American Political Science Review, 85*(2), 557–568.

Miller, Z., Burnett S., and Fram, A. (2019: September 15). Don't vote? The Trump campaign would like a word with you. *Associated Press*. Accessed online January 15, 2020: https://apnews.com/2c9022a09add4e5fbd501040c0d09d6f.

Montellaro, Z. (2019, May 6). *Political advertising could near $10B in 2020*. POLITICO. https://www.politico.com/newsletters/morning-score/2019/06/05/political-advertising-could-near-10b-in-2020-643200.

Morey, A. C. (2017). Memory for positive and negative political TV ads: The role of partisanship and gamma power. *Political Communication, 34*(3), 404–423.

Motta, M. P., and Fowler, E. F. (2016). The content and effect of political advertising in US campaigns. In *Oxford Research Encyclopedia of Politics*. Oxford University Press.

Nickerson, D. W. (2005). Partisan mobilization using volunteer phone banks and door hangers. *Annals of the American Academy of Political and Social Science, 601*(1), 10–27.

Nickerson, D. W., and Rogers, T. (2014). Political campaigns and big data. *Journal of Economic Perspectives, 28*(2), 51–74.

Nielsen, R. K. (2012). *Ground wars: Personalized communication in political campaigns*. Princeton University Press.

Noelle-Neumann, E. (1993). *The spiral of silence: Public opinion, our social skin*. University of Chicago Press.

Olson, M. (1965). *The logic of collective action*. Harvard University Press.

Panagopoulos, C. (2009a). Campaign dynamics in battleground and non-battleground states. *Public Opinion Quarterly, 73*(1), 119–129.

Panagopoulos, C., ed. (2009b). *Politicking online: The transformation of election campaign communications*. Rutgers University Press.

Panagopoulos, C. (2010). Are caucuses bad for democracy? *Political Studies Quarterly*, *125*(3), 425–442.

Panagopoulos, C. (2011). Thank you for voting: Gratitude expression and voter mobilization. *Journal of Politics*, *73*(3), 707–717.

Panagopoulos, C. (2013). Positive social pressure and prosocial motivation: Evidence from a large-scale field experiment on voter mobilization. *Political Psychology*, *34*(2), 265–275.

Panagopoulos, C. (2014). I've got my eyes on you: Implicit social-pressure cues and prosocial behavior. *Political Psychology*, *35*(1), 23–33.

Panagopoulos, C. (2015). All about that base: Changing campaign strategies in U.S. presidential elections. *Party Politics*, *22*(2), 179–190.

Panagopoulos, C. (2017). *Political campaigns: Concepts, context and consequences*. Oxford University Press.

Panagopoulos, C., and Endres, K. (2015). The enduring relevance of national presidential nominating conventions. *The Forum*, *13*(4), 559–576.

Panagopoulos, C., Larimer C. W., and Condon, M. (2014). Social pressure, descriptive norms, and voter mobilization. *Political Behavior*, *36*(2), 451–469.

Panagopoulos, C., and Francia, P. L. (2009). Grassroots mobilization in the 2008 presidential election. *Journal of Political Marketing*, *8*(4), 315–333.

Panagopoulos, C., and Weinschenk, A. (2015). *A citizen's guide to U.S. elections: Empowering democracy in America*. Routledge.

Panagopoulos, C., and Wielhouwer, P. W. (2008). Polls and elections: The ground war 2000–2004: Strategic targeting in grassroots campaigns. *Presidential Studies Quarterly*, *38*(2), 347–362.

Pierson, P. and T. Skocpol, eds. 2007. *The Transformation of American Politics: Activist Government and the Rise of Conservatism*. Princeton University Press.

Plutzer, E. (2002). Becoming a habitual voter: Inertia, resources, and growth in young adulthood. *American Political Science Review*, *96*(1), 41–56.

Poole, H., and, Rosenthal, A. (1997). *Congress: A political-economic history of roll call voting*. Oxford University Press.

Popkin, S. (1991). *The reasoning voter: Communications and persuasion in presidential campaigns.* University of Chicago Press.

Prior, M. (2007). *Post-broadcast democracy: How media choice increases inequality in political involvement and polarizes elections.* Cambridge University Press.

Repass, D. E. (1971). Issue salience and party choice. *American Political Science Review, 65,* 389–400.

Rhodes, J. H., and Albert, Z. (2017). The transformation of partisan rhetoric in American presidential campaigns, 1952–2012. *Party Politics, 23*(5), 566–577.

Ridout, T. N. (2009). Campaign microtargeting and the relevance of the televised political ad. *The Forum, 7*(2), 1–15.

Ridout, T. N., and Fowler, E. F. (2012). Explaining perceptions of advertising tone. *Political Research Quarterly, 65*(1), 62–75.

Ridout, T. N., and Franz, M. M. (2011). *The persuasive power of campaign advertising.* Temple University Press.

Ridout, T. N., Franz, M. M., Goldstein, K. M., and Feltus, W. J. (2012). Separation by television program: Understanding the targeting of political advertising in presidential elections. *Political Communication, 29*(1), 1–23.

Riker, W. H., and Ordeshook, P. C. (1968). A theory of the calculus of voting. *The American Political Science Review, 62*(1), 25–42.

Rosenstone, S. J., and Hansen, J. M. (1993). *Mobilization, participation, and American democracy.* Pearson.

Rove, K. (2010). *Courage and consequence: My life as a conservative in the fight.* Threshold Editions.

Rove, K. (2019, November 20). The campaign data arms race. *Wall Street Journal.* Accessed online March 1, 2020: https://www.wsj.com/articles/the-campaign-data-arms-race-11574294077

Schier, S. E. (2000). *By invitation only: The rise of exclusive politics in the United States.* University of Pittsburgh Press.

Schlesinger, R. (2018, December 26). Trump doesn't care about governing or being re-elected. He only cares about being popular with his base. *NBC News.* Accessed online March 1, 2020: https://www.nbcnews.com/think/opinion/trump-doesn-t-care-about-governing-or-being-reelected-he-ncna951956

Senate Committee on Commerce, Science, and Transportation. (2013, December 18).

Shaw, D. R. (1999). The effect of TV ads and candidate appearances on statewide presidential votes, 1988–96. *American Political Science Review*, *93*(2), 345–361.

Shaw, D. R. (2006). *The race to 270: The Electoral College and the campaign strategies of 2000 and 2004*. University of Chicago Press.

Shaw, D. R. (2008). Swing voting and U.S. presidential elections. In W. G. Mayer (Ed.), *The swing voter in American politics*. Brookings Institution Press. (pp. 75–101).

Smidt, C. D. (2017). Polarization and the decline of the American floating voter. *American Journal of Political Science*, *61*(2), 365–381.

Stolee, G., and Caton, S. (2018). Twitter, Trump, and the base: A shift to a new form of presidential talk? *Signs and Society*, *6*(1), 147–165.

Stuckey, M. (2005). Swinging the vote in the 2004 election. In R. Denton (Ed.), *The 2004 presidential election: A communication perspective*. Rowman and Littlefield. (pp. 153–166).

Taber, C. S., and Lodge, M. (2006). Motivated skepticism in the evaluation of political beliefs. *American Journal of Political Science*, *50*(3), 755–769.

Theriault, S. M. (2008). *Party polarization in Congress*. Cambridge University Press.

Thielman, S. (2014, March 31). What women watch on TV. *Adweek*. Accessed online March 1, 2019: https://www.adweek.com/tv-video/what-women-watch-tv-156621/.

Tiplady, S. (2019). U.S. presidential campaign strategy 1960–2012: Observing and explaining change in Rhetoric. PhD Dissertation. Keele University.

Todd, C., and Dann, C. (2017, March 14). How big data broke American politics. *NBC News*. Accessed online on March 6, 2018: https://www.nbcnews.com/politics/elections/how-big-data-broke-american-politics-n732901?cid=sm_npd_nn_tw_ma.

Turner, J. (2007). The messenger overwhelming the message: Ideological cues and perceptions of bias in television news. *Political Behavior*, *29*(4), 441–464.

Tynan, D. (2004, September 24). GOP voter vault shipped overseas. *PC World*. Accessed online September 2, 2019: https://www.pcworld.com/article/117930/article.html.

Tyson, A. (2019, June 19). Partisans say respect and compromise are important in politics—particularly from their opponents. Pew

Research Center. Accessed online January 5, 2020: https://www.pewresearch.org/fact-tank/2019/06/19/partisans-say-respect-and-compromise-are-important-in-politics-particularly-from-their-opponents/.

Van Boven, L., Judd, C. M., and Sherman, D. K. (2012). Political polarization projection: Social projection of partisan attitude extremity and attitudinal processes. *Journal of Personality and Social Psychology, 103*(1), 84–100. https://doi.org/10.1037/a0028145.

Vavreck, L. (2009). *The message matters: The economy and presidential campaigns*. Princeton University Press.

Walsh, K. C. (2004). *Talking about politics: Informal groups and social identity in American life*. University of Chicago Press.

Wayne, L. (2008, October 31). Democrats take page from their rivals playbook. *New York Times*. Accessed online March 1, 2019: https://www.nytimes.com/2008/11/01/us/politics/01target.html.

West, Darrell. (2013). *Air wars: Television advertising and social media in election campaigns, 1952–2012*. 6th ed. CQ Press.

West, Darrell. (2018). *Air wars: Television advertising and social media in election campaigns, 1952–2016*. 7th ed. CQ Press.

Westfall, J., Van Boven, L., Chambers, J. R., and Judd, C. M. (2015). Perceiving political polarization in the United States: Party identity strength and attitude extremity exacerbate the perceived partisan divide. *Perspectives on Psychological Science, 10*(2), 145–158.

Wielhouwer, P. (1995). Strategic canvassing by political parties: 1952–1990. *American Review of Politics 16*, 213–238.

Wilson, R. (2019, December 5). *Political ad spending set to explode in 2020*. The HILL. Accessed online March 1, 2010: https://thehill.com/homenews/campaign/473240-political-ad-spending-set-to-explode-in-2020.

Yourish, K. (2018, July 13). How Russia hacked the Democrats in 2016. *New York Times*. Accessed online January 3, 2020: https://www.nytimes.com/interactive/2018/07/13/us/politics/how-russia-hacked-the-2016-presidential-election.html.

Zagorski, M. (2020, February 25). Why marketers need to think addressable CTV—ASAP. *AdAge*. Accessed online March 1, 2020: https://adage.com/article/telaria/why-marketers-need-think-addressable-ctv-asap/2238751.

Zaller, J. R. (1992). *The nature and origins of mass opinion.* Cambridge University Press.

Zaller, J. R. (1996). The myth of massive media impact revived: New support for a discredited idea. *Political Persuasion and Attitude Change, 17,* 17–78.

INDEX

Note: Figures are indicated by *f* following the page number.

For the benefit of digital users, indexed terms that span two pages (e.g., 52–53) may, on occasion, appear on only one of those pages.